Reforming the Ruble

Monetary Aspects of Perestroika

Edited by Josef C. Brada
and Michael P. Claudon

NEW YORK UNIVERSITY PRESS
New York and London

Library of Congress Cataloging-in-Publication Data

Reforming the ruble : monetary aspects of perestroika / edited by
Josef C. Brada and Michael P. Claudon.
       p.   cm. — (Geonomics Institute for International Economic
Advancement series)
   Includes bibliographic references.
   ISBN 0-8147-1447-1
   1. Money—Soviet Union—Congresses. 2. Foreign exchange
problem—Soviet Union—Congresses. 3. Perestroika—Congresses.
4. Soviet Union—Foreign economic relations—Congresses. 5. Currency
convertibility—Congresses.   I. Brada, Josef C., 1942-   . II. Claudon,
Michael P.   III. Series.
   HG1075.R44   1990
   332.4'947—dc20   90-6573
                                                                          CIP

New York University Press books are printed on acid-free paper,
and their binding materials are chosen for strength and durability.

CONTENTS

Acknowledgments

Many have contributed to the success of this East-West venture. In the first place, this volume has benefited from the generosity of the conference sponsors: Jones International, Inc.; MMS International, Inc.; Pillsbury, Madison & Sutro; Robertson, Stephens & Company; and Scott-European Corporation. The conference also benefited from the participation of a large and diverse group of specialists on East-West relations. It included: Alexander Belov, Research Fellow, Institute for the Study of the USA and Canada; Jozef M. van Brabant, Chief, Centrally Planned Economies Section, United Nations; Josef C. Brada, Professor, Economics Department, Arizona State University; Michael P. Claudon, President, Geonomics Institute; James L. Cochrane, Senior Vice President, Chief Economist, New York Stock Exchange, Inc.; Joseph F. Furlong III, Partner, Robertson, Stephens & Company; Shirley Gedeon, Professor, Economics Department, University of Vermont; Robert Happeny, Partner, Booz-Allen & Hamilton; George R. Hecht, Chief Financial Officer, Robertson, Stephens & Company; George C. Kaiser, Chairman and Chief Executive Officer, Hanger Tight Company; Robert L. Krattli, President, Scott-European Corporation; Alexei Kunitsin, Senior Research Fellow, Institute for the Study of the USA and Canada; Krzysztof A. Lis, Polish Government Minister for Privatization, and Professor, School of Management, Warsaw University; Kalman Mizsei, Senior Fellow, Institute for World Economics, Hungarian Academy of Sciences; Thomas D. Moore, Professor of Management and Director of External Affairs, College of Commerce and Business Administration, University of Alabama; Vladimir Musatov, Head, Economics Department, Institute for the Study of the USA and Canada; Deborah Anne Palmieri, MacArthur Scholar, Center on East-West Trade, Investment, and Communications, Duke University, and Assistant Dean, The Graduate School, University of Southern California; Scott Pardee, Chairman, Yamaichi International America, Inc.; Peter J. Pettibone, Partner, Lord Day & Lord, Barrett Smith; Vladimir Popov, Senior Research Fellow, Institute for the Study of the USA and Canada; David Roberts, Assistant Vice President, Foreign Exchange, New York Federal Reserve Bank; Sandy Robertson, General Partner, Robertson, Stephens & Company; Vincent J. Ryan, Chairman, Schooner Capital; Francis Scotland, Senior Partner, Bank Credit Analyst, Ltd.; Rolf D. Schmidt, Director, Scott-European Corporation; Catherine Sokil, Assistant Professor, Economics Department, Middlebury College; Eric Stubbs, Center for Foreign Policy Development, Brown University; Graham Taylor, General Partner, Pillsbury, Madison & Sutro; and Nikolai Volkov, Head, Technology, Innovations, Production Company (TIPCO), and Head, Economics Department, Institute for the Study of the USA and Canada.

The staff of the Geonomics Institute, including Nancy Ward, Elizabeth Leeds, and George Bellerose, ably assisted in organizing and executing many aspects of the conference program. Colleen Duncan provided editorial assistance and shepherded the preparations of the volume for publication from the September 1989 conference through several stages of revisions, to this updated final version. Their contributions are invaluable.

                                                        The Editors

FOREWORD

> A revolutionary atmosphere reigns in the country. "The top" can't rule anymore and "the bottom" no longer wants to live in the old way. But revolution is revolution . . . . Like all revolutions, [however], the success of this one depends on how staunch and decisive the revolutionary forces are, on whether they can break the opposition of those who prefer obsolete social formations and structures.[1]

As of this writing, the revolutionary forces in the Soviet Union appear to be wavering. By May 1990, after five years of failed halfway measures, and facing demoralizing economic collapse, President Gorbachev still has not succeeded in clarifying how and when he wants to transform the planned economy into a market economy. Moreover, those favoring the stability and equality provided by communist central planning appear to be increasingly capturing the ear of the people on the street. As reported in the *New York Times*, Aleksei A. Sergeyev, a trade-union economist, insists the free-market proposals were "pregnant with social riot" and would lead to the overthrow of the government.[2]

Were that not enough, neither shock therapy nor any of the many gradualist marketization proposals can fundamentally alter the Soviet economic mechanism absent a complete overhaul of the Soviet financial mechanism. If the Soviet economy ever is to be a market-oriented one, the ruble and a related financial infrastructure must emerge as effective lubricants of economic activity. The economy must be monetized so that the ruble functions as a unit of account, store of value, and medium of exchange. As with marketization, ruble reform entails myriad fundamental and drastic mon-

1. Shmelev and Popov (1989).
2. Bill Keller, "Soviet Economy: A Shattered Dream," *New York Times*, May 13, 1990, p. A10.

etary changes, many of which will be poorly understood and thus threatening to entrenched bureaucrats and the populace alike.

The week-long conference from which this volume derives was co-sponsored by the Geonomics Institute for International Economic Advancement and ISKAN[3] in October 1989. This volume is the first of a two-part series focusing on the monetary aspects of economic reform in the Soviet Union. Its central goal is to make an initial in-depth examination of what reforming the ruble and monetizing the Soviet economy will entail. A companion volume, *Reforming the Ruble: Creating the Infrastructure,* growing out of Geonomics' May 1990 seminar, the title of which was Financial Markets, Joint Ventures, and Business Opportunities in the Soviet Union, will offer detailed menus of the practical steps to be taken if the ruble is to be reformed and the Soviet Union is to replace its failed system of central planning with one driven by the self-interest of buyers and seller.

This volume contributes exceptionally well to Geonomics' mission to bring together business leaders, government policymakers, and academicians. Geonomics seeks to promote initiatives that facilitate international business, and it sponsors and disseminates policy-oriented research and seminars. Geonomics is privately funded, nonpartisan, and not for profit. We welcome ideas and opinions for better achieving our goals.

Michael P. Claudon
President and Managing Director
Geonomics Institute

REFERENCES

Hewett, Ed A. 1988. *Reforming the Soviet Economy: Equality versus Efficiency.* Washington, DC: The Brookings Institution, p. 299.

Shmelev, Nikolai, and Vladimir Popov. 1989. *The Turning Point: Revitalizing the Soviet Economy.* New York: Doubleday, p. 293.

3. ISKAN is the Moscow-based Institute for the Study of the USA and Canada of the Soviet Academy of Sciences. Under a unique joint-venture agreement, our two institutes are working together to break down barriers to greater Soviet-American commerce.

INTRODUCTION

This volume grows out of the first workshop and third conference organized under the long-term agreement between the Geonomics Institute and the Institute for the Study of the USA and Canada of the Soviet Academy of Sciences. Held at the Geonomics House in Middlebury, Vermont, over three weeks in July 1989, the workshop produced the first multilateral plan for achieving ruble convertibility as early as the year 2000. The subsequent conference, which took place in October 1989, convened a dynamic mix of 40 business leaders, government officials, and scholars from the United States, the Soviet Union, and East Europe. They worked together intensively in three narrowly focused working groups to identify obstacles to doing business in the Soviet Union and to create practical proposals for their elimination.

I. WORKING GROUP FINDINGS

Ruble Convertibility

The working group analyzed the Geonomics ruble convertibility proposal. The five-phase plan, developed by Geonomics (see Chapter 5 in this volume), calls for a series of auctions that leads to convertibility by the year 2000. The working group reviewed the plan in light of the discussion and broad coverage it had attracted since being released in August. No substantive alterations were proposed to the plan's five-phase process. The group concluded that the slow pace of economic reform and the hoarding of rubles by Soviets represent the most significant obstacles to ruble convertibility.

Without major domestic price reform, the limited currency auction in the plan's Phase 1 will do little more than reflect the price distortions in the economy. For example, a manufacturing firm desperately needing western currency to buy computers might be willing to offer far more rubles per dollar than would be set by a true foreign exchange market. The group believes that the Soviet government must continue with price reforms even if the domestic political environment impedes a smooth transition.

The Soviet conferees estimated that as many as 300-450 billion rubles have accumulated in involuntary but highly liquid savings, largely due to consumer product shortages. Neutralizing or eliminating this "monetary overhang" is a vital element of successful domestic economic reform, and this element represents a particularly daunting challenge for the Soviet Union.

Two solutions were proposed, the first of which, offered by Soviet economist Vladimir Popov, came under heavy fire, particularly from his Soviet colleagues. Popov suggested importing US$20-30 billion in western consumer goods—financed by external hard currency borrowing—for resale within the Soviet Union. His colleagues argued that the inefficient Soviet economy was in greater need of high-quality manufacturing and technical goods, which must also be purchased with external borrowings.

The second approach, which called for the government to issue long-term savings bonds paying positive real interest rates, was more favorably received. New financial institutions, such as commercial banking and consumer credit, and a stock exchange would be required. A minority of the working group challenged the existence of an inflation-threatening ruble overhang, noting the existence of the second economy as a spending outlet for these rubles and citizens' willingness to take second jobs for increased employment.

These ideas merit careful consideration and further development, which will be accorded in Geonomics' May 5-8, 1990, conference on "Financial Reform and Doing Business in the Soviet Union and East Europe."

Doing Business in the Soviet Union

The working group on doing business in the Soviet Union, chaired by Scott-European Corporation President Robert L. Krattli, examined the factors that make the Soviet Union attractive to western business and evaluated obstacles to expanded U.S.-Soviet business activity. Soviet and American participants agreed that institutional problems exist on both sides of the Atlantic. However, the working group echoed a pervasive theme of the conference: real price reform is absolutely vital to making the Soviet Union more attractive to western business. The obstacles identified fall into three groups:

1. *U.S. Responsibility.* The working group stressed that the United States can easily remove the following barriers, certainly without full implementation of the major economic reforms the Soviets are attempting. Indeed, progress in the following areas will enhance Soviet reform efforts and thus will improve prospects for successful American business operations in the Soviet Union:

   a. grant most-favored nation status by eliminating the Jackson-Vanik Amendment. U.S. tariffs on Soviet goods are still levied at prohibitive Smoot-Hawley rates under the Jackson-Vanik Amendment. A strong consensus, bordering on unanimity, emerged that the Soviets had taken large enough strides in human rights to justify repealing Jackson-Vanik;

   b. ease highly restrictive export controls, established at least in part for political reasons, which unreasonably restrict U.S. high-technology exports to the Soviet Union;

   c. allow U.S. national banks and financial institutions, which have been closed out of the Soviet economy by restrictive regulations, to participate in loans or finance credits to the Soviet Union; and

   d. create greater awareness among American business leaders on how to conduct business in the Soviet environment.

2. *Soviet Responsibility*

   a. dysfunctional communications and distribution infrastructure in the Soviet Union, including the lack of telecommunications, roads, and convenient rail and air transport;

   b. the language barrier;

   c. absence of international accounting conventions;

   d. poor understanding of the time value of money and the resulting lack of positive interest rates;

    e. lack of a business culture;

    f. the Soviet attitude that joint ventures are simply selling the country to the capitalists;

    g. the bewildering array of prices, both legal and illegal, on the black and gray markets facing western joint-venture partners.

3. *Shared Responsibility*

    a. the inability to protect capital against currency devaluations, abrogation of joint ventures, or government expropriation. Capital protection guarantees were seen as absolute prerequisites to significant investment from the American side. The group pointed to the recently signed bilateral agreements between the Soviet Union and France and the Soviet Union and the Federal Republic of Germany as models to emulate.

The First Soviet-American Venture Fund

The working group laid the foundation for implementing a U.S.-based venture capital fund to channel approximately US$100 million into start-up and early-stage financing of Soviet technology enterprises.

Buoyed by the news that the First Hungary Fund has raised over $50 million for investment projects in that country, the discussion quickly turned to details of structure and implementation. The Fund will support high-technology, product-producing Soviet joint-venture companies. These companies will be entitled to preferential treatment under Soviet laws. There will be no requirement that all production occur solely in the Soviet Union or that the company be located in the Soviet Union. Joint-venture companies could be located at the optimal site for maximizing their success.

Western marketing and managerial expertise will be a key factor in assuring the success of the Fund's investee companies. U.S. and foreign managers and technical experts would assist investee companies as needed. The Fund management will consist of a board of directors, which will include Soviet participation yet U.S.-based control, to supervise an experienced U.S. venture capitalist who will direct fund investments. A U.S. fund administrator will be utilized. We expect that an international Big-Five accounting firm will be the Fund's auditor and accountant.

The long-term nature of investment projects in the Soviet Union favors at least a ten-year investment term. Therefore, a closed-end fund was preferred; subsequent investor subscriptions would be accepted later. The Fund envisages development of a liquidity mechanism for investors. The incentives given by the Hungarian National Bank with regard to liquidity options to the Hungary Fund are one approach.

The offering is anticipated to be US$100 million, with an investor minimum between US$500,000 and US$2 million and a six- to ninth-month selling period. Both U.S. and international venture capital investors, including individuals and corporations, will be sought. Attractive rates of return are expected to compensate for the high degree of risk and extensive management involvement of the Fund in investee companies.

II. MONETIZING THE SOVIET ECONOMY

The deliberations of the working groups and the discussions that precede the meetings of these groups focused on the monetary aspects of economic reform in the Soviet Union. This was in part due to the realization that the only way to dismantle a planned economy is to bring the existing system of arbitrary and distorted economic decisions under the discipline of a budget and realistic prices that would both require and create the conditions for rational economic decisions based on real tradeoffs among various economic objectives.

A second reason for stressing the monetary aspects of perestroika was the fact that restructuring the Soviet economy would require a massive infusion of foreign capital as well as the effective marshaling of the Soviet Union's own savings. Perestroika anticipates an upsurge in Soviet productivity and output, and ultimately in living standards as well. Such an upsurge, however, can only be brought about by retooling Soviet industry with new and productive machinery and equipment. Such machinery and the know-how to exploit it properly must come from the West, placing a heavy burden on the Soviet Union's balance of payments. The only way in which the Soviet Union can tap international capital markets now and repay its debts to the West in the future is if productive capacities created by perestroika are geared to the needs of western markets. Such a link can only be brought about by making the ruble convertible and by creating the possibilities for the effective transfer of western technology by means of new forms of business relations such as joint ventures.

Given the huge size of the Soviet economy, foreign capital can be a catalyst for progress, but domestic savings must finance the bulk of Soviet investment efforts under perestroika. To generate this volume of savings and channel it to the appropriate uses is a task that is beyond the old system of central planning. Increasingly, monetary channels and financial criteria must come into wider use.

Finally, however impressive the retooling of Soviet industry may be, it will be of no use to the Soviet economy if Soviet workers are unwilling to work. Inflation, both hidden and open, threatens not only to sap the willingness of the Soviet people to work, but, indeed, the social stability of the Soviet state. Thus, monetization and the submission to financial discipline are just as critical at the national level as they are at the level of the individual Soviet enterprise.

The Future of Socialism: Capitalism or a "Third Way"?

Th crisis in the Soviet Union and the socialist countries of East Europe is, of course, both political and economic. Indeed, political change has proceeded much more rapidly and has been much more extensive than has the transformation of the economic system. Moreover, because most of the political changes have been in the direction of creating a political system that embodies many elements of western democracy, including contested elections in a multi-party setting, the ascendancy of the rule of law over the arbitrary rule of the Communist Party and the emergence of parliamentary rule, observers have assumed that economic change must flow in the same direction. That is, with central planning discredited, the Soviet and East European economies are assumed to be moving in unison toward the creation of liberal market-directed and private-property-based economies.

In Chapter 1 of this book, Josef C. Brada warns against such an assumption. Comparing the current crisis in the Soviet bloc to the economic crisis of capitalism in the 1930s, he argues that, like capitalism, socialism may emerge from its crisis with more political change than fundamental dismantling of the socialist economy. While the absolute rule of the Communist Party may be rejected or at least weakened, its political competitors are also parties representing workers' interests. Thus, there is, at this time, no solid social or economic base for political parties seeking to restore private property as the dominant basis for economic activity. In Chapter 2, Robert V. Daniels delves more deeply into Gorbachev's social and political reforms, pointing to the fundamental changes that have been wrought in social life, in the role of the party, in ideology, and in the basic tenets on which Soviet foreign policy had been based. These great changes, whose historical antecedents and future implications Daniels ably sets out, stand in stark contrast to the as yet minimal progress in dismantling the Soviet planned economy.

Thus, we should not assume that the Soviet economy, or any of the East European economies, will follow the path toward the institutions and mechanisms found in the West staked out by political reforms. Once this dichotomy between economic and political reform is established, then the need for a greater sensitivity to the nuances of economic reform in the Soviet Union and a greater creativity in designing new institutions and mechanisms to guide the economy become clear. The remainder of the volume is devoted to such an analysis of Soviet economic reform.

Financing Perestroika

A key element of debates over the course and strategy of economic reform in the Soviet Union has been the question of how to create the financial equilibrium necessary for the success of any market-based economic reform. In a very real sense, these Soviet debates are very similar to the debates over tax policy and economic growth that preceded the Kennedy tax cut of 1964 in the United States. Like the Soviet Union, the United States was dissatisfied with its rate of economic growth, especially in light of the West European and Japanese economic miracles. Walter Heller, Kennedy's Chairman of the Council of Economic Advisors, argued cogently and persuasively that fiscal drag, in the form of excessively high taxes, was responsible for slow growth. Kennedy and Congress, however, were unwilling to cut taxes in an economy plagued by deficits resulting from a level of economic activity well below full employment. It was a tribute to Heller's political acumen and persuasiveness that he was able to convince both the President and the Congress that the tax cut, by raising the growth of GNP, would in fact be self-financing and actually would reduce the deficit in the long run.

In the Soviet Union, it is accepted by many economists that perestroika would increase output, incomes, and government revenues. The paradox is that such an improvement cannot be brought about without upfront financing to launch the reform. In Chapter 3, Vladimir Popov cogently poses the policy dilemmas facing Gorbachev. Some of Gorbachev's advisors urge a policy of extensive western borrowing, arguing that, like the U.S. tax cut of 1964, such loans will more than pay for themselves when the effects of perestroika make themselves felt, although their advice would surely be more compelling if they could agree on whether foreign loans should be utilized primarily for imports of machinery and equipment or for imports of consumer goods. Critics of these proposals argue that Soviet foreign debt is already too high, and the resource needs of perestroika should be met by shifting domestic resources from investment and defense spending to the consumer sector.

On the domestic side, the need for funds stems partly from the excessive share of GNP taken up by investment. Nearly 25 percent of GNP goes to investment, according to official Soviet sources, and Popov argues that this figure may be on the low side. In addition, there are other important claims for funds, including the need to create a viable social safety net for workers displaced by perestroika; the need to increase the provision of health and education service; and the need to deal with the Soviet Union's environmental crisis. With the government budget already in deficit, new funds are desperately needed.

Popov argues that the best policy for the Soviet Union is to borrow abroad to jump-start the reform process. Once the reform measures make themselves felt, he claims, many of the current liabilities will turn into assets. High levels of inventories, low capacity utilization, and the inefficient allocation of investment funds all represent "hidden reserves" that can be tapped by a successful reform program to produce dramatic improvements in output and growth. What is needed, according to Popov, is a leap of faith to get over the short-term financial obstacles to reform.

Whether the Soviet leadership is willing to take such a leap of faith depends in large part on how badly the Soviet economy fares under the current economic system and policies. Alexei Kunitsin argues in Chapter 4 that the near-term prospects for the Soviet economy are not good. The government has instituted a stabilization plan to deal with the current crisis, which has both a domestic and a foreign trade component. On the domestic front, the government deficit and the more rapid growth of wages than of consumer goods supplies constitute a volatile situation that the government hopes to ameliorate by retooling defense plants to produce consumer goods and by stimulating productive efficiency through some limited reforms.

Kunitsin argues that these measures are nugatory. Defense plants must be reconverted for civilian production, and workers must be retrained. The new reform measures are limited to only a few enterprises. In the meantime, industry is sliding into a critical situation characterized by a growing disorganization of relations between firms and their suppliers and a loss of government control over both commodity and financial flows. In the short run, Kunitsin argues, the situation is unlikely to improve and could deteriorate.

On the foreign trade front, the situation is little better. The external debt is growing, largely to cover interest payments, thus providing little relief to the domestic economy. Export revenues are vulnerable because they depend almost exclusively on fuels and raw materials, whose prices on world markets are falling. At the same time, the Soviet Union is critically dependent on key imports from the West, ranging from grain to machinery and advanced technology.

Kunitsin argues that in this desperate situation there are important opportunities for western business leaders because the Soviet Union will be forced into a closer integration with the world economy. Among the integration measures already adopted or

under active consideration are joint ventures, collaborative exploitation of Soviet technology, hard currency auctions, and free economic zones. Kunitsin notes that all these measures will require
start-up capital and thus in the short run will represent a drain on
scarce Soviet hard currency holdings. In the long run, however,
they will not only earn back this hard currency investment with
interest, but they will also contribute to the revival of a reformed
Soviet economy. Thus, as in the preceding contribution by Popov,
Soviet policymakers are urged on to further bold steps that carry
both short-term costs and the possibility of a big pay-off in the future.

Convertibility

The past several years have wrought tremendous and largely unexpected changes in the lives of the residents of the Soviet Union and
of the socialist countries of East Europe. In a very fundamental
sense, the essence of these changes has been to link the people of
these states to the social, political, and cultural life of the developed
market economies of West Europe, North America, and the Pacific
region.

On the political front, multi-party systems now exist *de jure* in
virtually all the East European nations and *de facto* in the Soviet
Union, where the Communist Party continues to maintain a
tenuous hold on its leading role in the face of an increasingly
independent legislature and the evolution of informal opposition
groups based largely on regional issues or specific concerns, such as
the environment. Therefore, by the end of 1990, virtually every
one of these countries will have elected a government through
genuine multi-candidate elections that are not dominated by a
single party.

Similarly, glasnost in the Soviet Union and the elimination of
state control over the media in East Europe have linked residents of
this region to the rest of the world culturally and intellectually.
Not only the facts, but opinions and the full range of cultural expression are freely available, both transmitted from abroad and
generated indigenously. Personal contacts between East and West
are also expanding, through old channels such as scientific, cul-

tural, and educational exchanges, and increasingly through more casual forms such as tourism.

These developments mean that the citizens of the socialist countries are rapidly becoming a part of western culture and democratic political practice. However, despite this cultural and political convergence between the two formerly antagonistic systems, there remains one fundamental way in which the citizens of East Europe and the Soviet Union continue to be as cut off from the rest of the world as they were in the darkest days of Stalin's terror. The missing link is the economic link, connecting the residents of one country with the needs and the output of their fellow human beings in other countries. The continuation of this barrier to economic contacts exists because of the inconvertibility of the ruble and the other currencies of East Europe into the currencies of other nations.

Because of this inconvertibility, the residents of the Soviet Union can think the same thoughts, create the same art, and enjoy similar political freedoms and responsibilities as do citizens of the West, but they cannot partake of the same goods, job opportunities, or economic rights because they have no means by which to decide about the consumption of foreign products or the export of domestic products. The inconvertibility of the ruble means that Soviet citizens can purchase only those foreign goods, and only in those quantities, determined by the state. This missing economic right to participate in the world market goes far beyond the ability to acquire the latest electronic gadgets, a pair of jeans, or a bottle of Scotch. Rather, it represents the right and the ability of citizens to link themselves with the world economy and to safeguard their most fundamental economic interests: to protect themselves against domestic inflation by acquiring foreign assets; to free themselves from dependence on monopolistic domestic producers; and to sell the fruits of their labor to the highest bidder on the world market. To live in a country with a convertible currency thus makes one as much an economic citizen of the world as free media and political rights unite one culturally and politically with the rest of the world.

The inconvertibility of the ruble and of the other socialist currencies is not, of course, imposed on the citizens of these countries without reason. Many of their industries are not competitive on world markets, their domestic prices are irrational and cannot serve as the basis for free trade, and they suffer from inflation and holdings of excess purchasing power in the hands of a goods-hungry population. To bring about convertibility, industries must be made competitive, markets must be made to function, and the value of the currency in terms of domestic goods must be maintained at a stable level. These requirements can be, and often are, viewed as insurmountable obstacles to convertibility of the ruble, and to most economists and policymakers in the Soviet Union they represent obstacles so great as to render convertibility a distant dream.

At the same time, it is evident that convertibility is the key to resolving most of these obstacles. A freely convertible ruble would establish an exchange rate at which Soviet goods, even manufactured goods, would be competitive on world markets. Moreover, it would create both the incentives for Soviet producers to adapt themselves to western markets and the conditions under which western capital and technology could assist them to raise their productivity and the quality of their products. Competitive markets would best be created with the assistance of imports from the West, which would quickly discipline domestic producers of shoddy goods and force improvements in the inefficient and inegalitarian distribution system that exists in the Soviet Union. Finally, the existence of a convertible currency would be the most effective control over the government's long-standing habit of financing its deficits by printing money. The need, then, is to devise creative ways of bringing about convertibility, not in an environment where all the preconditions for it already exist, but rather in an environment such as that of the Soviet Union, where these ideal conditions do not exist. By devising such an approach to convertibility, the strengths of the world economy can be brought to bear on the reform of the socialist economies.

The proposal for ruble convertibility contained in Chapter 5 is precisely this type of proposal. It takes both the distortions of the Soviet economy and the existing barriers to convertibility as given, and, working within the framework and timetable of Soviet reform measures, produces a phased and realistic plan for the gradual convertibility of the ruble by the year 2000. The program, developed by a team of Soviet and western economists during a three-week workshop at the Geonomics Institute in July 1989, represents one of the few concrete proposals that is both practical because it proposes a gradual program sensitive to the political and economic concerns of the Soviet leadership, and visionary because of its ability to achieve true ruble convertibility without requiring utopian measures.

In Chapter 6, Jozef M. van Brabant carefully spells out what true convertibility means and explains in considerable detail the relationship between current reform thinking and the possibility of making some or all of the CMEA currencies convertible. He also develops an innovative proposal for creating a form of convertibility among the CMEA members even if not all of them are able to achieve full convertibility against western currencies at the same time.

The need for a phased but relatively rapid transition to convertibility is underscored by Kalman Mizsei, whose contribution ably documents Hungary's external relations under the New Economic Mechanism (NEM), the reform measures begun in 1968 and extending to the present period. As Mizsei shows, the reform measures were imperfectly meshed with economic policy. This was largely the result of a lack of convertibility, which prevented the world market from correcting errors in monetary and fiscal policy and also left microeconomic reforms at an incomplete stage, with the Hungarian economy neither planned nor market directed. His analysis of a variety of extreme, and therefore utopian, approaches to making the Hungarian forint convertible surely suggests that something like the phased plan for ruble convertibility ought to be adapted to Hungarian circumstances.

Joint Ventures and East-West Capital Flows

During the period of the New Economic Policy (NEP), Lenin permitted western firms and entrepreneurs to operate and invest in the Soviet Union. Although these foreign concessions were not particularly large relative to the overall Soviet economy, they had about them an aura of the exotic and romantic, the mixture of two different economic systems, that lasted well beyond the end of the NEP in 1928. In East Europe, the ideological barriers to joint ventures with western firms, which rested on the Marxist notion that private owners of capital of necessity must exploit their employees, were first breached in Romania, then in Hungary and Yugoslavia, and subsequently in the other East European countries. Ideological purity, if not the logic of Marx's arguments, was retained by permitting the western participant no more than 49-percent ownership of the joint venture, though arrangements could be made to give the western partner a controlling role in business operations.

In quantitative terms, the economic benefits from this lengthy ideological debate were minor. As Krzysztof A. Lis and Henryk Sterniczuk show in Chapter 8, a total of 203 Polish joint ventures yielded US$220 million in foreign capital. Compared to Poland's external debt or to the volume of foreign direct investment in market economies of similar size and level of development, the results of Polish efforts to promote joint ventures are hardly worth discussing. Yet, the concept of joint ventures is potentially a viable and interesting one. In the current Soviet nostalgia for Lenin and the NEP period, it is also a topical issue because joint Soviet-western ventures are being touted as an important component of the foreign trade reforms that make up Gorbachev's perestroika.

Whether the Soviet Union can turn joint ventures into a useful tool of foreign economic relations remains to be seen, but the analysis of the Polish experience by Lis and Sterniczuk clearly spells out the most important parameters. The first key element is the law that governs the establishment and operations of joint ventures. Polish experience, like that of other East European countries, clearly shows the ethno- and system-centric nature of these laws. In general, the need to adapt to bureaucratic interference and inertia, to function within an alien and nonprofit-oriented economy, and to attempt to make profits in a system where profits are largely seen as the outcome of luck or influence rather than of rational activity are all simply pushed on to the foreign investor. This, of course, has the advantage of protecting the domestic system and the bureaucracy that operates it from risk and change, but it does little to stimulate the formation of joint ventures. Moreover, the potentially beneficial effect of joint ventures on the domestic economy is stifled because the domestic sector is effectively insulated from joint-venture operations.

In East Europe, joint ventures may well be overtaken by privatization and by expanded opportunities for foreign direct investment.

In the Soviet Union, such radical steps are not as yet viable options. Thus, the significance of the Lis and Sterniczuk paper is its message for Soviet policymakers to get their joint-venture legislation right. One way to do so would be for the Soviets to consider and adapt their laws to the needs of foreign business leaders rather than to those of Soviet bureaucrats.

Monetizing the Soviet Union: Banks, Bonds, and Stocks

The monetization of the Soviet economy will require the creation of new monetary institutions such as commercial banks. However, as Vladimir Musatov suggests in Chapter 9, the creation of banks alone cannot change a socialist economy based on planning to an economy subject to monetary and price signals. If one follows his thinking to its conclusion, it is possible to argue that monetization, and even the creation of real banks, will not be possible without a realignment of property rights away from the state and in favor of individuals, either in their roles as workers or as citizens.

In the traditional Soviet economy, the State Bank was not a banking institution in the strict sense. It took in government deposits and the deposits of the population and issued credits to enterprises. In contrast to western banks, which have capital at risk and must make decisions about the creditworthiness of potential borrowers, the State Bank issued short-term credit on demand and long-term loans at the behest of the central planners. While Musatov is correct when he says that bankers recognized "the unsound nature of the loans they extended," it is noteworthy that neither the existence of the unsound borrowers nor the bank's capital were at risk. Indeed, there were no nonperforming loans. To understand why bad loans could be made with no negative consequences for either the lender or the borrower, it is only necessary to realize that the borrowers, as state enterprises, could not fail and thus could not default on their loans. Moreover, the State Bank, with no real capital at risk, was little more than a disbursing and collecting agent for the state.

Musatov explains the current reforms in Soviet banking, which seek to establish the State Bank as a true central bank, while lending to enterprises devolves to five specialized banks owned by the state and to commercial banks established by single or several cooperatives or enterprises.   The five state-owned banks are handicapped by the fact that they have inherited the old "unsound" loans of the State Bank, but as long as the borrowers are state-owned enterprises whose property cannot be seized for failure to repay these loans and whose losses are covered by state subsidies, the nature of banking has not changed.   In contrast, the emerging commercial banks do have capital at risk, but there are nevertheless dangers in this form of banking structure.   In addition to those dangers mentioned by Musatov, the Yugoslav experience with enterprise-owned banks suggests another.   In that country, loss-making enterprises issue commercial paper that is accepted by other enterprises and ultimately by banks, but rather than being covered by the issuing enterprise, these promissory notes are monetized by banks seeking to prevent the enterprises that own them from going bankrupt.   The result is, of course, inflation.

One way of creating borrowers who can default on their loans and thus impose losses on careless lenders is through privatization. Musatov's discussion of the issuance of stocks and bonds by Soviet enterprises shows what a slow and complicated process this is likely to be.   Musatov points out that the Soviet Union's policy of forced bond sales in Stalin's time has discredited them as a financial instrument, forcing Soviet enterprises to rely on stock issues instead. The issues of stock undertaken to date in the Soviet Union do not establish any property rights.   Indeed, they appear to be little more than a scheme to provide good workers with rewards without running afoul of regulations on the growth or differentiation of wages.   Stockholders have no voting rights, and the stock must be resold to the enterprise when workers retire or leave the firm. Indeed, the right to own stock is tied directly to employment, and the magnitude of the dividend payment may be related to work performance.   Thus, these new "owners" neither control what they own nor can they dispose of it freely.   Worse yet, one of the principal characteristics of stocks—their ability to change in value in response to market perceptions of the capitalized value of the firm's future earnings—does not exist, and thus the ability of the capital market to allocate capital is severely circumscribed.

It is in part on the basis of these considerations that Musatov argues that Soviet state enterprises increasingly must be converted to corporations. However, in the absence of a price reform, the efficiency implications of such a move are questionable. If enterprises lose money because they are run inefficiently or make large profits because their products are in high demand, then capital flows reflecting such data serve to make the economy more efficient. On the other hand, if enterprises lose money because the price of their inputs is kept low by subsidies, then capital flows responding to these signals need not lead to any improvement in efficiency.

III. CONCLUSIONS

The upshot of the conference discussions and the papers in this volume is that small steps toward reform and toward the expansion of East West economic relations must always be in progress. Without a succession of such small but practical measures, there can be no improvement in the Soviet Union's economic condition and in its trade with the United States. Indeed, in cases such as the convertibility proposal, small steps can ultimately lead to large results. At the same time, virtually every paper in this volume stresses that this host of small steps must be embedded in a framework that provides guidance and coordination between the small steps in one area of the economy and those in another. Thus, such small steps in convertibility as hard currency auctions eventually must be supported by progress in price reform and enterprise autonomy. The expansion of Soviet enterprises' trading rights must be marked by the willingness of western business and financial leaders to develop mechanisms, such as the venture fund established during this conference and described earlier, that can turn the potential freedom of Soviet firms into concrete transactions with the West.

To take effective small steps requires entrepreneurship and business acumen on both sides, and these ingredients were provided by the business participants at this conference. The weaving of these small steps into a coherent march forward is the task of the academic participants. The bringing together of these two groups is the goal of the Geonomics Institute, and we thank them all for their energy and insight.

Josef C. Brada
Michael P. Claudon

APPENDIX A

Time constraints made it impossible to complete a Fund prospectus during the conference. However, the Geonomics Institute and the Soviet-based Technology, Innovations, Production Company (TIPCO) signed a protocol to continue pursuing this project in Moscow. A delegation comprised of representatives from the Geonomics Institute; Pillsbury, Madison & Sutro; and Robertson, Stephens & Company traveled to Moscow in December 1989 to review potential investment targets and to continue negotiations leading to a targeted implementation of the First Soviet-American Venture Fund in the spring of 1990.

The First Soviet-American Venture Fund

The U.S.-Soviet working group concluded the following in connection with the formation of a Fund:

1. The history and development of venture capital in the United States was reviewed. The structure and nature of international venture capital funds were then discussed. Extensive discussion ensued on the types of U.S.-Soviet projects suitable for investment by the Fund. High technology, originating from premier Soviet institutions, was selected as the most suitable target for Fund investment.
2. Specific potential projects were reviewed. The typical Fund investee will be a Soviet joint-venture company, which will be entitled to preferential treatment under Soviet laws. Such joint ventures will focus on the production and export of internationally competitive products to world markets.
3. American marketing and managerial expertise will be a key factor in assuring success.
4. Attractive rates of return are expected to compensate for risk and extensive management involvement of the Fund in investee companies.
5. Investment opportunities will be screened by Soviet groups and then presented to the Fund.

6. The percentage of Fund ownership may be greater than 50 percent and will be set on a case-by-case basis, depending on the contributions of the Fund and the Soviet side.
7. There is no requirement that all production must be done in the Soviet Union, it being contemplated that joint-venture companies invested in by the Fund may be located in the United States, Canada, or other countries, wherever it is optimal for the success of the investee company.
8. Soviet ministry approval for technological licenses abroad ordinarily will be forthcoming.
9. The Fund envisages development of a liquidity mechanism for investors, with minimum lock-up periods and expiration dates.
10. A closed-end fund is preferred, with subsequent investor subscriptions being accepted after the demonstration of success.
11. Rather than a limited life fund, the long-term nature of investment projects militates in favor of a longer-term vehicle.
12. Discussions centered on the excellent potential of Soviet free trade zones and technology parks as optimal locations for investee companies' operations. The U.S. participants noted the benefits to investee companies resulting from close geographic connections to leading Soviet academic institutions.
13. Soviet taxation of investee companies will be mitigated by reason of the priority high-tech nature of operations, it being noted that joint ventures enjoy a two-year tax holiday and other ancillary Soviet tax benefits.
14. Concerning management structure, experienced U.S. venture capitalists will direct Fund investments, subject to the supervision of a board of directors (including Soviet participation). A Fund administrator located outside the United States will be used. The auditor and accountant to the Fund is intended to be an international Big-Five accounting firm.
15. The offering is anticipated to be a minimum of US$100 million with an investor minimum between US$500,000 to US$2 million and a six- to nine-month selling period.
16. Both U.S. and international venture capital investors (including individuals and corporations) will be sought.
17. General (and Soviet, in particular) risk factors associated with the Fund were discussed and will be explained to investors.

18. Given the high profile of the Fund, there will exist a need to ensure that the public-relations dimension of Fund operations in the Soviet Union is adequately covered. The cost of these operations to the Fund is not expected to be significant in aggregate.

19. The impact of U.S. legal constraints on technological transfer was discussed, but it was not considered to be a materially detrimental factor.

20. Fund investors will not be subject to U.S. taxation at a fund level. International investors are not to be subject to U.S. income tax on the gains derived from the Fund's operations.

21. Expert U.S. and foreign managers, as well as technical experts, will be located by the Fund and transferred to the Soviet Union to assist investee companies as needed, it being recognized that western production control and general management and international marketing expertise will likely be required for investee companies to succeed; it being also recognized that Soviet managers will thereby gain transferred expertise, which will be of general use in the development of the Soviet economy.

22. The Soviet participants invited a working group, under the auspices of the Geonomics Institute, to visit Moscow to review potential investment targets, with a view to the early implementation of a prototype U.S.-Soviet venture capital joint-venture technology company, together with TIPCO before the end of 1989.

APPENDIX B

This working group also concluded negotiations and drafted a protocol, signed by Geonomics and TIPCO, to establish a Geonomics Soviet Management Training Program. The draft reads:

> To facilitate Soviet-American trade, commerce, and joint ventures, TIPCO and the Geonomics Institute announce their intentions to found and administer a joint program to train international business executives.

> To develop a plan for this training program, TIPCO invites four representatives of Geonomics and two American business executives, chosen jointly by TIPCO and Geonomics, to Moscow for one week in November 1989, and Geonomics invites four TIPCO professionals or specialists to Middlebury in the spring of 1990.

> The training program will concentrate on internationally accepted principles of accounting, advertising, banking, corporate and labor law, economics, management, marketing, and trade, as well as education in the culture and history of each nation.

The Reforms Placed:
An Historical Perspective

CHAPTER 1 _____

Crisis and Reform in East Europe and the Soviet Union

JOSEF C. BRADA

There is a sense of impending crisis gathering about East Europe and the Soviet Union. There is speculation in the West about the possibility of economic collapse. There is serious contemplation of the consequent social and political changes in these countries and of their democratization and conversion to market economies to avoid the crisis. Observers in the Soviet Union and East Europe are similarly pessimistic. There, many economists believe that the existing system has run its course, and they vie with each other to catalogue its shortcomings and to offer ever more radical solutions for resolving the crisis. We are, of course, too close to these events, as actors or spectators, to understand the historical import of these developments. Yet they are of such significance that we must try to distance ourselves from them to gain some perspective on the possible pace, nature, and extent of reform.

Join me in contemplating a concrete situation: consider a large country, potentially rich and productive, but whose economy is in disarray, whose production is well below capacity, whose workers suffer from the resulting shortages of goods and services, and whose productive potential is consequently wasted. Take into account the following:

This chapter is a lightly edited version of the keynote speech delivered at the Geonomics Conference in Middlebury, Vermont, October 1989. No effort has been made to conceal the informality of the oral presentation.

1. Faith in the economic system wanes. Economists, politicians, and the media argue that the system is not viable in the long run, that it cannot sustain growth and technical progress, and that the government's role in the economy must change.
2. Trade relations are also in disarray, in part because the country's trading partners are afflicted with the identical malaise and in part because of the large capital flows among them.
3. Economic difficulties give rise to new political movements that challenge the political orthodoxy with new and often extreme and divisive views.
4. The country is led by a dynamic leader who proposes to restore economic prosperity by curbing the power of the country's financial and industrial leaders. He is resisted by parts of the government and by individuals in industries. He obtains scant support from a dispirited and apathetic population.

   What is this country and who is its leader? If you chose Mikhail Gorbachev's Soviet Union in socialism's hour of crisis, you are correct. If you chose Roosevelt's America in the Great Depression, capitalism's hour of crisis, you are also correct. It is this parallel that I wish to explore. What can we learn from the crisis of capitalism? What can it teach us about the current crisis of socialism?

TWO THEORIES OF CAPITALISM'S CRISIS

The sources of the Great Depression remain controversial, but there are two main hypotheses. The first argues that the Depression marked the climacteric of a system of laissez-faire capitalism that had slowly evolved and come to dominance in the 100-plus years between 1815 and the start of the Great Depression. This view, perhaps put forward most compellingly by the economic historian Karl Polanyi, sees the crisis and demise of the system as inevitable. Capitalism, Polanyi argued, was inconsistent with human social needs:

> The origins of the cataclysm lay in the utopian endeavor of economic liberalism to set up a self-regulating market system. The pe-

culiarity of the civilization the collapse of which we have witnessed was precisely that it rested on economic foundations. All types of societies are limited by economic factors. Nineteenth century civilization alone was economic in a different and distinctive sense, for it chose to base itself on a motive only rarely acknowledged as valid in the history of human societies and certainly never before raised to the level of justification of action and behavior in everyday life, namely, gain.[1]

If we accept the hypothesis that the Great Depression resulted from the fundamental flaws of laissez-faire capitalism, then we must expect that the new system would be clearly different and improved.

The second hypothesis argues that the Great Depression created an economic and social crisis, a crisis of faith in capitalism and an intellectual crisis. However, the Depression ultimately resulted from a conjuncture of the ordinary workings of the capitalist business cycle with serious policy mistakes. Among these policy mistakes were the unwillingness of the United States to assume from Britain the role of world banker, the effort of many countries to maintain the gold standard in the face of destabilizing capital flows, and inept, if not counterproductive, monetary and fiscal policy.

If these were the sources of the Depression, then recovery required only minor corrections in the system, and laissez-faire capitalism could continue with undiminished vigor.

ECONOMIC POLICY CHANGES WROUGHT BY THE DEPRESSION

Criteria for comparing and analyzing pre- and post-Depression capitalist economies are not immediately clear and are beyond the scope of my talk. Let me, rather, take Polanyi's list of major systemic changes wrought by the Depression and briefly examine how his analysis has stood the test of time. He highlighted three major changes: (1) the destruction of the gold standard; (2) the change from laissez-faire to state-controlled capitalism; and (3) the end of the balance-of-power system of international relations.

1. Polanyi, Karl. 1944. *The Great Transformation.* New York: Rinehart and Company.

First, the gold standard was believed to be critical to the inter-
nationalization of laissez-faire capitalism. Without the restrictions
of a gold standard, trade and capital flows could not effectively discipline national economic policies and maintain the dominance of
market forces over national labor and money markets. After
World War II, the market economies unsuccessfully attempted to
reconstruct this mechanism through the Bretton Woods system.
But the demise of the gold standard and even of the Bretton Woods
system of fixed exchange rates has not been a tragedy. Indeed, one
can argue that the existing system of flexible exchange rates for
some countries and pegging rates for others has led to an interna-
tionalization of the world's market economies that was never
achieved under the gold standard. Credit for the expansion of international trade is only partly due to this systemic change; technology and the expanded role of the multinational firm must also
share the credit in this evolution. Nevertheless, the momentous
import attributed to the demise of the gold standard, as well as the
costly efforts to restore it, seem, in retrospect, misplaced. Indeed,
the exchange rate system that has replaced it is seen by many as
achieving the same, if not greater, benefits at lower cost.

Second, conventional wisdom argues that the state had to assume
greater responsibility for the macroeconomic stability and control
of an unregulated market economy. Nevertheless, several points
should be borne in mind. First, the change required the development of a theory to support such intervention, which was provided
by Keynes and his followers. This change also required developed
economies whose financial markets, taxes, and government purchases could sustain Keynes's extensive monetary and fiscal policies. Finally, although government involvement varies greatly
among market economies, the past decade has seen a sharp reduction in many countries in the scope of government intervention in
the economy. Whether the rise of state-regulated capitalism is a
revolutionary or an evolutionary change remains an open question.

Third, despite Polanyi's assessment, the balance-of-power system
appears alive and well. While international relations have been
changed by the development of nuclear weapons, ideologically
based blocs have coalesced around the two superpowers.

Thus, if capitalism was in crisis in the 1930s, then the institutional and systemic changes needed to overcome the crisis are in

retrospect much less revolutionary than thought at that time. Surely capitalism remains an international, market-based system that is motivated by gain. This leads to two conclusions: crises of economic systems need not presage radical change; and the Great Depression was not the great climacteric of a failed system, but a policy-induced crisis that was largely overcome by more appropriate policies.

The implications for the crisis of socialism are thus clear: First, we need to analyze carefully whether the crisis results from a conjuncture of bad policy and exogenous events or from inherent defects in the system. Second, we must be cautious in our expectations of extensive change. The burden of proof is, I would argue, on those who predict such radical change.

THE CASE FOR A CRISIS OF SOCIALISM

Socialism rejects the unregulated market's total domination over social life and the concept of individual gain as the principal objective of society. The rejection of these principles will be complete, communist theorists argue, only under full communism. Nevertheless, there are some common socialist denominators:

1. Markets, if they exist, are instrumental, not dominant. Planners view markets as tools, much as they do directives, orders, and laws. Consumer preferences in the marketplace do not influence economic outcomes.
2. Economies of socialist countries have been decoupled to a large extent from international markets—especially qualitatively, if not quantitatively.
3. Individual incentives exist, but social solidarity, in the form of the right-to-work and job security, predominates.
4. Aggregate growth has replaced individual gain as the objective of the system.

In what sense is this system in crisis? How, by its very nature, is it unable to fulfill its goals? As the principal goal is growth, we may begin there. Socialist economies have a creditable growth record over the post-World War II period, but serious problems loom behind that record. Most important has been a marked and growing deceleration of growth, beginning in the late 1950s. Some socialist economies are now stagnant.

Growth has resulted mainly from increased inputs and investment rather than from increased factor productivity through the development and use of technology. Growth has been very costly and has required that these countries devote a disproportionate share of their gross national product to investment. This investment has limited the ability of these economies to meet consumer needs. In contrast, growth in capitalist economies comes largely from increased factor productivity and technology. The qualitative decoupling of these economies from the world market has led to distorted economic structures, particularly a hypertrophy of the industrial sector. This overexpansion of the industrial base has limited gains in total factor productivity and has led to overconsumption of material and energy.

The consequent need to restructure these economies endangers job rights. If labor is to become a "commodity" subject to the discipline of the market, then the communist system's fundamental logic is destroyed. This marketization of the system or the rewriting of the social contract is much more than that phrase implies. It may be that such a contract cannot be rewritten unless the new terms include changes in property rights and in the political monopoly of the Communist Party. Such changes imply fundamental and extensive changes in the system.

To many observers the elimination of job rights and the implicit emergence of market control, as opposed to social control, of the right to work breaks down the barriers to market control over all other aspects of economic activity. Simultaneously, if the right to work is to be allocated by a market, however influenced by the state, then there is no reason workers should surrender control of the mechanism for making economic policy to the Communist Party. A single-party state is incompatible with the functioning of a national market and its regulation by the state. Thus, reform in many of the socialist countries leads to a marketization from which political pluralism must follow. But, it is not clear that marketization of the extent suggested here is necessary, or that marketization and political pluralism must lead to extensive privatization.

Before exploring the inner as opposed to the outer limits of economic reform, let me examine the hypothesis that the crisis of socialism is the result of a conjuncture of external shocks and poor internal policy, and that the system does not need a major revamping. In putting forward this hypothesis, I recognize the resistance it is likely to meet from western observers of socialist economies and even more from observers from within those economies. Nevertheless, I believe that their arguments result partly from mass psychology, which is now very negative, perhaps much more so than events warrant.

I would like to remind you of the track record of economic growth in West Europe. From 1978-1982, West European unemployment averaged 6.1 percent and GNP grew at 2.3 percent per year. What were the popular perceptions? In the first period, West Europe was perceived as the sick man of the international economic system. "Eurosclerosis" had set in. Structural change and growth in Europe were blocked. The inability to foster structural change in turn was leading to the increasing "technological irrelevance"—and thus also the economic and cultural irrelevance—of Europe.

Now, however, with worsened employment performance and marginally better growth performance, the West Europe of 1992 and its constituent countries are the object of unbounded enthusiasm if not euphoria among both foreign and European observers. Lack of structural change and technological obsolescence have been replaced by stories detailing European entrepreneurship, design, and product quality.

A reverse trend may be at work in the case of the Soviet Union and East Europe. From 1983-1987, Soviet GNP grew by only slightly less than 2 percent per year and net material product (NMP) by 3.4 percent per year. In East Europe, NMP grew by 4.2 percent per year. Comparatively, these are not bad results. True, they mask objectively worsened conditions in some countries. But economic conditions in Poland and Hungary were created by serious policy mistakes in foreign borrowing. The Soviet Union faces inflationary pressures that stem from inflationary financing of the government deficit and from wage increases far in excess of gains in productivity.

This is not to argue that there are no objective reasons for popular dissatisfaction or that such dissatisfaction does not exist. Plainly it does, it is widespread, and it affects how people view the economic and political system and their willingness to work. Nevertheless, these negative perceptions need not be interpreted as the sources of a fundamental breakdown of the system. Moreover, a change in psychology, at least in some countries, could sharply reduce the pressure for change in the system.

WHAT CHANGES ARE NEEDED?

What are the minimum political changes needed to see the system through its crisis? Some countries will need a measure of pluralism, largely because the Communist Party cannot preside over a liquidation of past mistakes single-handedly. At the same time, new parties, representing workers' interests against the marketization of labor, are more likely to be interested in the distribution of the cost of structural change between workers and the communist bureaucracy than in sweeping privatization. Any nascent bourgeosie that develops will most likely come from the ranks of the party and the industrial managers. In other countries, past mistakes may be less egregious and can be liquidated under a party government. This is most likely in those countries, like the Soviet Union, where the legitimacy of the Communist Party rests on its own efforts and has not been imposed by Soviet power. It is possible in some cases that the privileges and advantages of party membership will come under pressure, but such privileges will not be entirely overturned.

Economic changes may also be minimal. With workers' parties defending against the marketization of labor, structural change will be slowed, and privatization will only touch the periphery of industry. Social control over employment will be maintained even as the economy is restructured and opened to the world. Thus, a minimal set of reforms will leave the leading role of the Communist Party intact in some countries, while in others power may be shared with parties whose interests also lie in the demarketization of labor. These parties will also prefer economies that rely more on planning than on markets to set economic objectives.

Consequently, we should not assume that the current developments in the Soviet Union and in East Europe presage either the demise of socialism or the transformation of these states into market economies and smoothly functioning pluralistic democracies. Such a transformation is possible but not necessary. This transformation will require an act of political will that is not yet evident among parties opposing the Communists.

CHAPTER 2

Gorbachev and the Soviet System: An Historical Perspective

ROBERT V. DANIELS

It has become obvious to all but the most obdurate skeptics that the reforms initiated in the Soviet Union under the leadership of Mikhail Gorbachev represent no mere tinkering with the Soviet system, but rather an attempt at fundamentally redirecting what had manifestly become an obsolete political and economic structure. Whether the effort will succeed against the resistance of conservatives and amid conditions of economic crisis is another question, as is the question of how and why Gorbachev managed to undertake such a radical reform. To find the answers, we must consider how the Gorbachev era fits into the whole perspective of the Soviet regime's historical development.

As we look first at Gorbachev's own time in office, it appears that he did not conceive of his reform program all at once. Certainly, its enunciation only unfolded step by step, probably in response to events and problems as they emerged. In its initial presentation at the April Central Committee Plenum in 1985, perestroika was indeed no more than tinkering, though it was based, as Gorbachev himself reported, on considerable discussion beforehand with intellectual critics of the old system (Gorbachev 1989). In this first phase, Gorbachev was doing little more than to resume the reform program of Brezhnev's immediate successor as General Secretary, Yuri Andropov, who served from November 1982 to February 1984. After the conservative respite under Konstantin Chernenko, who served from February 1984 to March 1985, Gorbachev began by reemphasizing Andropov's strictures on discipline, incentives, and the acceleration of economic development within the framework of the old system, not to mention the celebrated anti-vodka campaign.

Roughly a year after becoming General Secretary, Gorbachev seemed to have decided on a major new departure, centering on the concept of glasnost. There is plenty of evidence, some from Gorbachev himself, that he was encountering serious resistance in the party apparatus and in the central economic bureaucracy, in opposition even to the modest Andropovite reforms he was pursuing up to that time. I suspect also that revelation of the initial cover-up of the Chernobyl disaster had something to do with his change of heart. Gorbachev evidently decided to seek an entirely new political base for the reform program, one outside the recalcitrant bureaucratic apparatus that had been the foundation of political power in the Soviet Union since Stalin's rise in the 1920s.

Gorbachev's new strategy was to turn to the intelligentsia as a social force and to liberate the press and the writers as instruments to prod reform along. Change in Soviet society would now be achieved not by administrative directives, but by unleashing the intellectuals to exert freely the pressure of informed opinion.

Unfortunately, glasnost did not put an end to the political and economic difficulties standing in the way of Gorbachev's reform program. In economics, following the advice of liberals such as Abel Aganbegyan, Director of the Institute of Mathematical Economics in Novosibirsk; Leonid Abalkin, Director of the Institute of Economics in Moscow; and Nikolai Shmelev, Senior Associate of the Institute for the Study of the USA and Canada in Moscow, he quickly came to the conclusion that incentives and exposés within the old structure were not enough. He would have to expand the meaning of perestroika to include the fashioning of an entirely new model of socialism, returning to the New Economic Policy (NEP) of the 1920s for its inspiration. Central ministries and planning organs would be shrunk in favor of heavy reliance on market relationships and an ever-widening sphere for individual and cooperative enterprise. This approach bore fruit in, among other things, the law on enterprises that took effect in January 1988. Moscow was soon awash with cooperative restaurants offering western-style service and western-style prices. Agriculture would be radically reorganized by decentralizing the collectives and encouraging family and small-team work units on a contract basis—a reform that Gorbachev proceeded to implement vigorously. Industry, on a selected but cumulative basis, was directed to shift to the principle of "economic accounting" *(khozraschot)* and self-financing.

Politically, glasnost and the expanded interpretation of perestroika seem to have prompted sharply intensified resistance to Gorbachev, not only in the party apparatus and government bureaucracy, but among the blue-collar workers as well. Evidently, he had difficulty maintaining firm reformist majorities in the Politburo and the party's Central Committee, despite his leadership shakeups in 1985 and 1986. In reaction to the unfolding of Gorbachev's program, a new split appeared both in the Politburo and further down in the party. Now the disagreement was not between Brezhnevites and reformers because the former had been discredited and cleaned out, but between reformers of the early Andropovite variety and reformers of the bold Gorbachevian stripe. It appears that even when Gorbachev elevated younger members of the party apparatus, they turned cautious at the prospect of radical change and a diminution in their own institutional power. In response to the conservative challenge forming around Second Secretary Yegor Ligachev (an Andropov protegé), Gorbachev adopted a new strategy to broaden his power base. He had scheduled an All-Union Party Conference for June 1988—the first such mid-term mini-congress since 1941—to advance the reform program. However, he was balked by the party apparatus over delegate selection; the republican and provincial officialdom preferred the time-tested method of slate-rigging to assure conservative dominance of the meeting. Gorbachev made the momentous decision to break with the usual practice and go directly to the party rank and file to challenge the *apparatchiki* in genuine party elections. He was in effect attacking the historic base of leadership power in the party.

The result of Gorbachev's defiance of the apparatus was less than an unqualified success. It generated much confusion and acrimony, even to the point of public demonstrations when some local officials countermanded the results of party elections. But though he managed to get delegate seats for a few of the reformist intellectuals, independently of the bureaucratic responsibilities that had become the traditional prerequisite for selection, Gorbachev seems by and large to have failed in his principal design.[1] While no statistics are available, it appears that a substantial majority of the Conference delegates was the product of the old system of manipulated selection on the basis of bureaucratic office-holding.

To be sure, the residual weight of the party apparatus did not prevent the Nineteenth Party Conference from becoming an extraordinary medley of independent voices, more so than any party gathering since the early 1920s. On the other hand, while Gorbachev got the resolutions he wanted on constitutional and economic reforms, there was no progress on basic questions of power, including the restaffing of the Central Committee that he had initially hoped for.

This setback enhanced the political importance of another side of Gorbachev's program, the plan verbally endorsed by the Conference to shift substantial power and responsibility, both central and local, from the party as such to a strengthened presidency (soon occupied by him) and to the hierarchy of central and local soviets. To my mind, the shift from the party toward the state gave the latter a real political status it had not had since the Russian Civil War. By broadening Gorbachev's power base, the new arrangement lessened his dependence on the unreliable party apparatus. In any case, the new emphasis is interesting because, like glasnost, it called into question not only the basic political development of Stalin's time—the dominance of the party apparatus—but also the central principle going back to Lenin—the hegemony of the Communist Party.

While pursuing his growing reform agenda and fighting off the challenge of the conservatives, Gorbachev simultaneously began to recast some of the Soviet regime's basic principles in matters of ideology. He soft-pedaled all the familiar Marxist categories, starting with the proletariat, in favor of higher "humanist" values, and he embraced what amounted to the interest-group analysis favored by North American political scientists, to take cognizance of all the functional and occupational groupings that make up any modern society (Gorbachev 1988a). "Socialist pluralism" became the new

---

1. See Radio Liberty Research, RL238/88, June 5, 1988; RL237/88, June 8, 1988; and RL242/88, June 10, 1988.

byword (Gorbachev 1987a). Gorbachev's supporters were allowed to challenge the long-standing party monopoly in communications and intellectual life; scholars at the Institute of Marxism-Leninism, for example, spoke to me explicitly of abjuring their old role of ideological control and instead merely exercising "initiative" in the context of a "normal intellectual life." Anticipating the East European drama of the following year, some of Gorbachev's people openly acknowledged the parallels with the Czechoslovakia of the Prague Spring.[2] All this meant the end of Marxist-Leninist-Stalinist dogma, both as a system of thought and as a vehicle for imposing intellectual conformity.

The cult of Lenin survived for a time, but Lenin's image was itself modified through the old technique of selective quotation. Soviet publicists played down the fanatical Lenin of the Revolution and the Civil War and played up the pragmatic Lenin as he improvised during his first months of power and again as he expressed himself in his last, cautionary, even pessimistic writings while lying ill in 1922-1923.[3] Lenin would hardly recognize himself in this latter day picture—he would find that the most fundamental premises of his thought, including the supremacy of (alleged) class values, the class criterion of ethics, the equation of the party and the proletarian mission, and the party's monopoly in public political discussion, were all being abandoned.

Gorbachev's break from tradition in foreign policy, under the rubric of "The New Thinking," drew a contrast with the rigid and confrontational attitudes of his predecessors that needs no elaboration. Obviously, economic considerations were a powerful motive in this, but the extent to which the "new thinking" went beyond the old dogmatic myths and rationalizations bespeaks a basic new political factor as well. The history of Stalin's devious conduct of foreign affairs, along with his domestic crimes, finally began to be acknowledged for what it was—"hegemonistic great-power ambitions," in the words of one Soviet scholar (Dashichev 1988). The

2. See Krivosheyev (1988). Krivosheyev was an *Izvestiya* correspondent in Prague at the time of the Soviet intervention. Shortly afterwards, the Soviet Ambassador to Italy, Nikolay Lunkov, made a similar statement (Radio Liberty Research, RL412/88, September 6, 1988, p. 4).

3. See, for example, "Reading Lenin: More Democracy," *Pravda*, April 22, 1988 (*Current Digest of the Soviet Press* 40, 17: 1-5, May 25, 1988). See also Keller (1987).

new thinking went so far as to recognize that Soviet hyper-defen-
siveness and even Soviet maintenance of conventional force superi-
ority was actually counterproductive, contributing as it did to the
hostility of foreign governments (see, for example, Kondrashev
1988). By 1989, the new thinking even extended to the repudiation
of the "Brezhnev Doctrine" in East Europe, and Soviet acceptance—
even encouragement—of the extraordinary political chain reaction
that toppled one hard-line communist leader after another.

Gorbachev and his people have called into question some of the
most fundamental ideological postulates of Soviet foreign policy, including the irreconcilable confrontation with capitalism, the class
struggle dimension in international relations, and the mission of
national liberation in the Third World.[4] "The backbone of the
new way of thinking," Gorbachev wrote in 1987, "is the recognition of the priority of human values, or, to be more precise, of hu-
mankind's survival . . . . We deemed it no longer possible to retain . . . the definition of peaceful coexistence of states with different social systems as a 'specific form of class struggle'" (Gorbachev
1987b, 146-47). With the end of radio jamming, the relaxation of
entry and exit controls on individuals—even émigrés—the solicita-
tion of joint ventures with foreign business enterprises, and steps
toward convertibility of the ruble, the Soviet Union moved a remarkable distance, if not all the way, toward behaving like a modern country—if you will, like a bourgeois country.

Given the depth and centrality of the political and ideological
changes he introduced, it is little wonder that Gorbachev aroused
misgivings and worse among the party professionals who had
been trained throughout their careers to insist on discipline and
conformity. Nevertheless, he appeared to have overcome the long
stand-off with the conservatives when he successfully brought off the
palace coup of September 30, 1988, the "September Revolution," as
some Soviet intellectuals called it. Reverting to the oldest methods
of Muscovite conspiracy, Gorbachev carried out a successful preemp-
tive strike against his adversaries to cut their influence without actually trying to destroy them. Most important among the steps he

---

4. See, for example, the interview with V. I. Dashichev, "The Paths that Are
Chosen for Us," in *Komsomolskaya Pravda,* June 19, 1988 (*Current Digest of the Soviet
Press* 40, 26: 29, July 27, 1988).

took was the clear downgrading of Second Secretary Ligachev by relegating him to the traditionally junior position within the Secretariat of responsibility for agriculture (Gorbachev's old job).

ELECTIONS OF MARCH 1989: A TURNING POINT

Constitutional changes that Gorbachev pushed through in the summer and fall of 1988 were at first greeted with skepticism or even misgivings, seeming as they did to enhance his personal power by giving him a much-strengthened position as President of the Soviet Union in addition to his party leadership. In reality, Gorbachev was preparing another step, the most momentous of all, in search of a broader base of power independent of the party apparatus. By encouraging contested elections to the new People's Congress and allowing free campaigning (insofar as he could impose these rules on reluctant provincial officials), Gorbachev threw open the door to a genuine, if imperfect, democratic process. This was the turning point for many Soviet citizens, a time when they suddenly began to feel free. Gorbachev was sharply criticized for reserving one-third of the Congress, 750 seats, for "social organizations," including 100 seats for the central party leadership and token workers and peasants, but, in fact, this functional allocation actually widened the opportunity for leading intellectuals, writers, and scientists, including Andrei Sakharov, to win seats. The results of the ballot on March 26, 1989, were astounding: dozens of radical critics and reformers elected, official candidates defeated in many places, and some local bosses running on the old-style, single-name ballot defeated by "none of the above" when more than 50 percent of the voters crossed their names off.

Subsequent developments confirmed the democratic momentum. National TV brought live broadcasts of the sessions of the Congress in May and June to the entire Soviet populace, treating them to a spectacle of political give-and-take such as the Soviet Union had never known except for the reform years around 1905. When the Congress, pursuant to the Constitution, chose the new Supreme Soviet from among its own members to do the actual legislating, there was a momentary let-down because the provincial conservatives in the majority excluded many of the best-known reformers

from the higher body. Nevertheless, the Supreme Soviet belied expectations and proceeded to function as a genuine parliament,
rewriting and even defeating government legislative proposals
and on occasion refusing confirmation to government nominees
for the cabinet. There had been a profound shift in the nature and
locus of power, and even in the behavior of some communist conservatives when they found themselves in a position of genuine
legislative responsibility.

Largely overlooked in all this excitement were further steps
Gorbachev took to wrest control of the now demoralized party machine away from the conservatives. In April 1989, he secured the
resignations of the numerous "dead souls" on the Central
Committee—members who had been removed from the bureaucratic positions that entitled them to membership—and promoted
as many new people as the rules would permit. He struck again at
the Politburo level in September, removing the long-time
Ukrainian boss Shcherbitsky and two other conservatives and promoting still more backers of reform. The chances of an organized
conservative coup within the apparatus seems to have been broken
up for good.

TOTALITARIANISM AND ITS LIMITED LIFE SPAN

If Gorbachev's reforms, superficial though they may have been at
first, grew into a quest for a fundamental redirecting of Soviet society, how was such a turnabout possible within the doctrinaire and
totalitarian framework of Soviet politics? Further, what are the
implications of the Gorbachev "revolution" for our overall under-
standing of the Soviet experience and the concept of totalitarianism?

While I believe that the much-abused concept of totalitarianism
is still valid as a description of the Stalin era, the totalitarian system has had both a beginning and an end, historically speaking.
Its rise in any country is directly and exclusively connected with
revolution—or counterrevolution—though it emerges full blown
only at a late stage in the revolutionary process, after the characteristic revolutionary surge of fanaticism and mass mobilization and
civil war has spent itself. In other words, totalitarianism is the

characteristic twentieth-century form of post-revolutionary dictatorship.

But totalitarianism does not then become immutable, contrary to the celebrated doctrine formulated by Professor Jeane Kirkpatrick (1979), who later served as President Reagan's Ambassador to the United Nations.   The collapse of Stalinist Communism in East Europe, once the threat of Soviet intervention no longer backed it up, has consigned this notion to the dustbin of academic history. Even before the dramatic autumn of 1989, examples abounded among communist countries of the softening or decay of totalitarianism.   By the 1980s, Yugoslavia and Hungary could not be described as anything more severe than "authoritarian."   In 1968, Czechoslovakia demonstrated the possibility of the dismantling of totalitarianism from within, and Poland in the Solidarity years of 1980-1981 showed that totalitarianism could be overthrown by a sufficiently determined society.   It follows that even in the Soviet Union, when the time became ripe, totalitarianism would be subject to these possible developments, even without the shock of military defeat that ended Nazism in Germany and fascism in Italy.

A recapitulation of Gorbachev's revisions of Stalinism and even Leninism demonstrates how far and how fast he moved toward dismantling the structure and the psychology of totalitarian control.   He challenged, of course, the Stalin model of the centrally planned and bureaucratically administered economy, calling it the "braking mechanism."[5]   In the spirit of a neo-NEP symbolized by the rehabilitation of Nikolai Bukharin, the whole structure of the economy fashioned by Stalin in the course of the collectivization and five-year plans of the early 1930s was rejected, even though disputes continued over the actual material progress that the country made in this period.   Going further, Gorbachev rejected the primal Leninist bias against petty-bourgeois enterprise, especially in services and agriculture, the nationalization of which is so universally inappropriate and counterproductive.   He urged "democratization" and "mass participation" in industrial administration in terms that, if they are to be taken seriously, approached the

---

5.   The phrase "braking mechanism" was coined by Tatyana Zaslavskaya in "Report on the Necessity of a Deeper Study in the USSR of the Social Mechanism of the Development of the Economy," *Arkiv Samizdata*, A55043, August 26, 1983. It was translated as "The Novosibirsk Report" in *Survey* 27: 99, 106, Spring 1984.

semi-syndicalist philosophy of the Workers' Opposition of 1920-1921, which fought vainly against bureaucracy and for "collective management" (Kollontai 1921). He held out for the ideal of socialism, but he sought to redefine it in ways that would fundamentally change its nature.

In politics, Gorbachev called into question the most fundamental elements of the Soviet system, namely the role and structure of the Communist Party. While adhering to the constitutionally exclusive position of the party, he abandoned the ideals of "iron discipline" and "monolithic unity" that Lenin imposed during the Civil War and in the fateful resolution against factions adopted by the Tenth Party Congress in 1921. He challenged the domination of the party by the apparatus that dates from the 1920s, with almost the same arguments that Trotsky used in protesting the emergence of machine politics under Stalin: "The bureaucratization of the party apparatus has developed to unheard of proportions by means of the method of secretarial selection" (Trotsky 1943). He rejected the party's direct administrative domination over the civil government of the soviets that has prevailed since that same Civil War era, with arguments about the separation of powers that sound remarkably like the idealistic opposition to Lenin's centralism.

Continuing his efforts to relocate the center of power, Gorbachev carried through his constitutional change to permit genuine, if still restricted, elections, unparalleled in the Soviet Union since the abortive election of the All-Russian Constituent Assembly a few weeks after the Bolsheviks took power in 1917. This concession implicitly opened the way toward the possible evolution of a pluralistic and *de facto* multi-party political system such as Communist Russia had not seen since the outbreak of civil war in the summer of 1918. Together with this fundamental political shift, Gorbachev surrendered the Communist Party's last word in cultural and intellectual life, which had been imposed by Stalin in that crucial period of the early 1930s.

Other areas of policy evidenced the same deep revisionism under Gorbachev. In foreign affairs, he moderated the confrontationist approach in Soviet Russia's relations with the outside world that distinguished the country's behavior ever since the Allied Intervention of 1918-1920, indeed ever since the Bolshevik Revolution. At the risk of a major political explosion and Russian nationalist backlash, he tolerated a growing spirit of self-expression among the national minorities, calling a halt only where independence movements or hatreds between different minorities threatened to get out of hand. He spoke of a *Rechtstaat*—"a state governed by the rule of law"—and made promises to keep the secret police under wraps and to respect the legal rights of individuals to a degree not heard since the Revolution (Gorbachev 1988b).

In sum, in terms of policy directions, Gorbachev took the country all the way back not only to the pre-Stalin era, but to the earliest months of Lenin's rule, before the Civil War, before the attempt to communize the entire economy, before the imposition of the Communist Party's total political monopoly. There was a short period then, from the October Revolution to the spring of 1918, before the wrenching and hardening experience of the Civil War and War Communism, when the outlook of the new Soviet regime was substantially more cautious and more pluralistic than it became later, and when revolutionary politics were still highly decentralized and spontaneous. At the outset, Lenin warned his followers, "Socialism is not created by decrees from above. Statist bureaucratic automatism is alien to its spirit" (Lenin 1917). The difference in the 1980s is that Gorbachev was orchestrating a return to the earliest forms of Soviet power from the top down, but under much more stable circumstances, without the fanaticism, revolutionary passion, and pure chaos that destabilized the earliest version of the Soviet experiment.

Is there any explanation for the remarkable and quick transformation of the contemporary Soviet political scene under Gorbachev, other than the benevolent and practical judgment of the man in charge? Is there some logic inherent in the post-revolutionary dictatorship and its totalitarian manifestation that destines that trying phase of a country's experience to come to an end? The record of certain other communist countries suggests that there may indeed be such a natural tendency.

Real revolution, of course, is not an instantaneous event, rather, it is a prolonged process, carrying a country through successive phases of moderate protest, radical revolt, and pragmatic consolidation. Russia experienced the escalation of its revolution in 1917-1918 from benign democratic hopes to fratricidal violence, and then to the utopian fanaticism of the War Communism epoch of

1918-1921, all of which was followed by the retreat and stock-taking of the NEP era from 1921-1928. What succeeded the NEP ought to be recognized as a further and distinct phase in the revolutionary process: the emergence of post-revolutionary dictatorship.

Personified in the Soviet instance by Joseph Stalin, the post-revolutionary dictatorship represents an opportunistic synthesis of the revolutionary and the traditional. The revolution survives in the rhetoric and legitimation of the post-revolutionary regime; the traditional reasserts itself in the resumption of autocratic methods and nationalistic ambitions under the new labels. Most ironic about Stalin's regime was his ability to identify this course with the revolution, and to convince most of the world, friend or enemy, that he was still the champion of the brave new ideal. He accomplished this by holding on to the institutional forms and vocabulary of socialism, while turning their social and cultural content into the opposite of what the socialist movement had traditionally fought for. Under Stalin, Marxist ideology became a new form of "false consciousness," used to legitimate a regime that had strayed far—perhaps inevitably so—from its early principles.[6]

STALIN'S NEW CLASS: AN OPPRESSIVE BUREAUCRACY

Critical Marxists, in the Soviet Union or outside, have always had a hard time explaining the Stalin phenomenon in the traditional class terms of Marxian analysis. They could not accept Stalin as the embodiment of the proletariat, but his program after 1929 obviously did not represent a bourgeois or petty-bourgeois restoration. The answer ultimately was the theory of the "New Class," that is, a society dominated by the new bureaucracy, independently of private property ownership. Refining this notion, we can say that Stalinism rested both on the ruling bureaucracy (appropriately sifted by the purges) and on the less creative or "technical" part of the intelligentsia, while it could only suppress or emasculate the more creative elements of the intelligentsia.

6. I have developed this proposition in a paper, "Stalinist Ideology as False Consciousness," to be published in the Proceedings of the Fourth International Colloquium of the Feltrinelli Foundation, Cortona, Italy, 1989.

Reform since Stalin has been driven or at least supported by the extraordinary revival of the creative intelligentsia, first under Khrushchev and more recently under Gorbachev. Unfortunately for Khrushchev, he did not proceed far enough or consistently enough to mobilize this segment of society as a basis for reform. In the course of the 1960s and 1970s, however, the creative intelligentsia grew more numerous, more necessary, and more influential—in a word, more "dominant."[7] It was ready, when Gorbachev decided to unleash it, to emerge as the key force backing the reconstruction of the Soviet system. In essence, Gorbachev turned to the dominant class, the intelligentsia, to mobilize it against the old, recalcitrant ruling class.[8]

Stalinism had an economic basis and a cultural basis, as well as the direct support of compliant bureaucrats and functionaries. Economically it was one answer—not the best answer, we know now, but one logical answer—to the challenge of backwardness and industrial development and the needs of military power. However, the centralized planned economy remained a logical answer only in the early stages of the attack on these problems, and Stalin did not implement it very rationally. Now it has clearly become counterproductive, and this fact is the original reason that drove Gorbachev in the direction of radical reform. Culturally, Stalinism was supported by some of the oldest and deepest attitudes among the less westernized elements of the Russian people, rooted in centuries of serfdom and backwardness and reinforced by 70 years of barracks socialism. Millions of people expected centralized autocratic rule; felt comfortable in the knowledge of a *"krepkii khoziain"*—a tough boss—at the helm; avoided the kind of low-level initiative and responsibility that a complex modern economy depends on; and felt at home with the cult of secrecy and the compulsion to present a prettified image of the country to the outside world.[9] All of these elements are still frequently articulated by Soviet conservatives. The cultural factor remains a major obstacle to the successful pursuit of perestroika in both the political and economic realms.

7. In the sense proposed by the Yugoslav philosopher Svetozar Stojanovic (1981).
8. For an amplification of this argument, see Daniels (1988).
9. See Keenan (1986); Daniels (1987).

CAN THE "MODERATE" REVOLUTION BE REVIVED?

Counterrevolution, open or covert, is not the end of the revolutionary process. Despite natural historical foundations, such as those
that supported Stalinism, counterrevolutionary practice remains too
much at odds with a nation that has previously experienced the
hopes and excitement of a revolution. It cannot persist indefi-
nitely. As the current Soviet crisis demonstrates, counterrevolutionary dictatorship stands in the way of what the nation, or its politically effective elements, still knows it is capable of. At some
point of vulnerability, usually when it experiences reverses in war
or a crisis of succession, the post-revolutionary regime is rejected.
There follows a revival of the philosophy and power arrangement
of the early, moderate phase of the revolution. This "moderate revolutionary revival," as I have termed it, appears to be the natural
resolution of the accumulating tensions, frustrations, and failures
that a nation suffers under its post-revolutionary regime.[10]

Can the concept of the moderate revolutionary revival be applied
to Soviet Russia? There are, in fact, two episodes in the post-Stalin
era that appear to qualify, at least in their potential: the era of reform under Gorbachev, and its forerunner during the heyday of
Nikita Khrushchev.

In his condemnation of Stalin's crimes, his relaxation of the
party's pseudo-revolutionary dictates in intellectual life, and his
gestures toward the revival of egalitarianism, Khrushchev was in
fact moving in the direction of the moderate revolutionary revival.
Unfortunately, he failed to question the economic institutions of totalitarianism established during the early Stalin years or the corresponding political institutions of apparatus rule formed earlier.
As a result, the moderate revival under Khrushchev turned out to be
abortive—a first in the history of post-revolutionary regimes.
Khrushchev failed because he did not develop an independent social base for reform apart from the party apparatus, and the apparatus remained committed in its own interest to the principles of the
Stalinist dictatorship. To be sure, Khrushchev had the natural support the intelligentsia, but the intelligentsia remained physi-

10. See Daniels (1988, 127-33), in which I have detailed the concept of the
"moderate revolutionary revival."

cally at the mercy of the conservatives. The apparatus had little difficulty in subduing independent thinkers or driving them underground after the political ground started to crumble under Khrushchev.

Upon the demise of the Brezhnev generation, and with the Khrushchev precedent in mind, another effort to bring about the moderate revolutionary revival was not only logical but predictable (Daniels 1985, 362-65). This is the real historical significance of Gorbachev's restructuring. In the perspective of the Russian Revolution and the country's long post-revolutionary travails, perestroika is a fundamentally new step, opening a qualitatively new era in the history of the Soviet Union. Gorbachev called it a "revolution." In a sense this is true, although in the broader revolutionary scheme it is only the last phase of that long and onerous process.

The Soviet Union's moderate revolutionary revival under Gorbachev did not immediately become irreversible. Conceivably, Gorbachev's unfolding campaign for democratization could still be aborted, as Khrushchev's reforms were, given the residual political power of the party apparatus. Soviet intellectuals have been very sensitive to the danger. As history shows, the moderate revival is a difficult time, when the relaxation of coercion liberates enemies of compromise both on the Left and on the Right.

I have tried here to outline one way of looking as a historian at recent Soviet developments, to recognize what is old and what is new and the logic that connects them. Naturally, there are limits to Gorbachev's reconstruction of the Soviet system. He had neither the intention nor the capability of turning the Soviet Union into an image of the United States. For one thing, he hung on religiously to the concept of socialism, whatever the actual content he may have invested the term with.

Evaluating Gorbachev's Soviet Union and his model of socialism runs the familiar hazard of the two extremes. On the one hand, recognizing his progress toward the political values that most westerners now share, it is easy to be carried too far by wishful thinking. On the other hand, some have found it convenient to deny that any fundamental change has taken place, or could take place, and thereby evade the difficulty of rethinking old, originally well-founded but now outdated premises and stereotypes.

I believe that Gorbachev's reforms, enduring or not, have posed a major new intellectual challenge to western Sovietology. This is nothing less than rethinking most of our premises for the under-standing of the Soviet system. If we look objectively we can see the applicability of all our basic models—of the economy (the command system), of the political system (totalitarianism), of international behavior (Cold War bipolarity), of the ideological system (Marxist-Leninist orthodoxy)—dissolving right before our eyes. These are models in which western Sovietologists may have invested entire careers. So we face a challenge to our ways of thinking about the Soviet Union that is in a way analogous to the challenge now being experienced by the Soviet conservatives, faced as they have been with the fact that all their mental furniture has gone out of style.

Recognition of this need to rethink does not mean that all our previous conceptions are meaningless and irrelevant. The Soviet Union as we used to understand it has become history, but it still remains as history. As such, the old Soviet picture is just as relevant to the new processes of the present as any other aspect of the Russian historical legacy. It is the point of departure for the changes initiated under Gorbachev, as well as the basis for under-standing the profound difficulties and uncertainties that still lie in the way of the Soviet Union's new course. Keeping in mind the limits of the old model, we must now go on in our respective fields to try to define and understand what the Soviet Union came to in the 1980s and into what uncharted seas it may be headed.

REFERENCES

Daniels, R. V. 1985. *Russia—The Roots of Confrontation.* Cambridge, MA: Harvard University Press.
——. 1987. "Russian Political Culture and the Post-Revolutionary Impasse." *The Russian Review* 46: 2, April.
——. 1988. *Is Russia Reformable?* Boulder, CO: Westview Press, pp. 53–74, 105–126.

Dashichev, V. I. 1988. "The Search for New East–West Relations." *Literaturnaya Gazeta*, May 18 *(Current Digest of the Soviet Press* 40, 24: 4, July 13).

Gorbachev, M. S. 1987a. Speech to leaders in the media and the creative unions, July 10, as reported in *Pravda*, July 15. Cf. Radio Liberty Reports, RL280/87, July 16.

——. 1987b. *Perestroika: New Thinking for Our Country and the World.* New York: Harper & Row.

——. 1988a. Report to the 19th All-Union CPSU Conference, *Pravda*, June 29 *(Current Digest of the Soviet Press* 40, 26: 20-21, July 27).

——. 1988b. Report to the 19th All-Union CPSU Conference, *Pravda*, June 28 *(Current Digest of the Soviet Press* 40, 26: 19-20, July 27).

——. 1989. Speech to a meeting of scientists and cultural figures, as reported in *Pravda*, January 8 *(Current Digest of the Soviet Press* 41, 1: 2-3, February 1).

Keenan, E. L. 1986. "Muscovite Political Folkways." *The Russian Review* 45: 2, April.

Keller, B. 1987. "Kremlin Reinterprets and Re-emphasizes the Legacy of Lenin." *New York Times*, May 10.

Kirkpatrick, J. 1979. "Dictatorships and Double Standards." *Commentary* 68, 5, November.

Kollontai, A. 1921. *The Workers' Opposition.* Chicago: IWW.

Kondrashev, S. 1988. "Conventional Forces." *Izvestiya*, April 2 *(Current Digest of the Soviet Press* 40, 14: 11, May 4).

Krivosheyev, V. 1988. *"August 1968."* *Moscow News* 35, 28, August.

Lenin, V. I. 1917. "Answer to a Question of the Left SRs" (Central Executive Committee, November 4). *Sochineniya* 22: 45. Third edition. Moscow: Marx-Engels-Lenin Institute, 1928-1937.

Stojanovic, S. 1981. "Marxism and Democracy: The Ruling Class or the Dominant Class?" *Praxis International* 1, 2, July.

Trotsky, L. 1943. Speech to the Central Committee and the Central Control Commission, October 8, 1923. In Leon Trotsky, *The New Course.* New York: New International, p. 154.

Perestroika and the Demand for Capital

CHAPTER 3

Perestroika and the Demand for Capital in the Soviet Economy

VLADIMIR POPOV

One of the most widely debated issues of the current Soviet economic reform program is the demand for foreign capital over the course of perestroika. Academic economists and politicians, Soviet as well as western, differ greatly on how best to meet this demand. Some argue strongly in favor of heavy foreign borrowing to finance an immediate increase in consumer goods imports, which they see as vital to the success of perestroika (Shmelev 1989). Others argue that borrowing be used to finance increased imports of machinery and equipment for the consumer goods industry. In addition to keeping foreign borrowing from becoming permanent, less borrowing would be required, making the debt easier to repay, as the increased production of consumer goods will substitute for imports, thus allowing a foreign currency savings (Shatalyn 1989).

There are those who oppose the idea of foreign borrowing altogether, although on different grounds. Interestingly enough, among those who are against foreign borrowing are the so-called market-oriented economists (Abalkin 1989; Aganbegyan 1989; Latsis 1989), as well as the nonmarket-oriented economists (Antonov 1989; Kosolopov 1989). Some of them argue that external financing of either consumption or investment is dangerous now because the Soviet international indebtedness is already high, and that the need for more consumer goods should be met by shifting both domestic and import spending away from investment goods and toward consumption goods, an approach that more or less falls in line with the official Soviet government position at the moment.

The same differences in attitude toward foreign borrowing are apparent in the analysis of western specialists. Many of them (for example, Padma Desai, Ed Hewett, and Jan Vanous) strongly support the idea of external financing of the Soviet economy.[1] But other western academicians and politicians oppose financing perestroika by external credits because doing so will weaken the stimulus for domestic economic restructuring while allowing the Soviet government to postpone radical reforms and cuts in military expenditure. Also, sometimes it is remarked that the inflow of foreign capital may ease the financial constraints that are badly needed now for Soviet enterprises and the government, and that the associated inflow of consumer goods will create strong competition for the Soviet traded goods sector, which may suppress potential Soviet exports to the West (McKinnon 1989). In short, the issue of foreign capital in today's Soviet economic development is a highly controversial one, and current vigorous debates certainly reflect the crucial character and importance of the issue.

The purpose of this paper is to evaluate the overall demand for capital in the Soviet economy and the possible role of foreign borrowing in meeting this demand. Section I deals with the structure of national income (the relative shares of consumption and investment). It is argued that a transition to a market economy—provided that reforms are truly radical—will possibly substantially reduce the absolute size and relative share of investment in national income, simultaneously increasing the size and share of the consumption fund.

Section II examines reasons additional funds are urgently required, particularly focusing on the need to reduce the government budget deficit and to increase expenditure for social and welfare programs necessary to ease the burden of economic restructuring.

Finally, Section III compares various solutions to meet the demand for additional funds. It is argued that neither the cuts in investment, the increase in prices, nor the monetary reform can be regarded as acceptable ways of financing the pressing economic

---

1. *New York Times*, July 31, 1989.

and social expenditures. The preferable route is external borrowing, which would allow the Soviet Union to make the transition to an efficient market economy at a low cost and without a considerable reduction in living standards. Borrowing abroad is certainly a temporary solution, as the international indebtedness of a country cannot grow endlessly. Therefore, it makes sense to proceed with foreign borrowing only if simultaneously decisive steps are undertaken to implement radical market-type reforms. At the same time, provided that radical economic restructuring is under way, external financing seems to be the only solution to meet the inevitable costs of adjustment during the transition to a point where perestroika will pay for itself.

I. CAPITAL INVESTMENT IN THE SOVIET ECONOMY

Soviet economic data, as is well known, are incompatible with western statistics, rendering it difficult to estimate not only the demand for capital in the Soviet economy, but also the relative size of actual capital investment. Official Soviet statistics exclude all service industries and calculate the national income only in those industries in which material products are manufactured. The Soviet State Statistical Committee recently began to publish GNP data, but the sectoral breakdown of GNP is still unavailable.

The data on investment, national income, and GNP are presented in Table 3-1. Table 3-1 shows that the share of accumulation (which is the analogue of net investment) in national income fluctuated in the range of 24-26 percent in recent years. In 1988, the ratio of gross capital investment to GNP was approximately 25 percent, and gross nonresidential capital investment was 21 percent of GNP. Compared to other countries, these are very high shares. In the United States, for example, net investment (gross investment less depreciation) averaged 6-7 percent of national income in the 1980s. The substantial difference is partly explained by the exclusion of the service sector from Soviet calculations of national income. Estimated Soviet national income for all industries in 1987 was 700-750 billion rubles.[2] When compared to the United States, the share of net investment in national income should be about 20 percent. Thus, even with this recalculation, the difference is still enormous: 6-7 percent in the United States, and close to 20 percent in the Soviet Union.

The same holds true for the indicators of the share of gross investment in GNP, which in 1980-1985 was 15 percent in the United States; 18-21 percent in the United Kingdom, West Germany, and France; and 30 percent in Japan. The comparable figure was 25 percent in the Soviet Union in 1987. Similarly, the share of non-residential investment in GNP was 11 percent in the United States; 14-16 percent in the largest West European countries; and 25 percent in Japan. It was 21 percent in the Sovet Union.[3] Some Soviet economists point to statistical discrepancies in official calculations of investment, national income, and GNP, resulting largely from the use of inappropriate, artificially set prices, from indirect taxes and subsidies to influencing prices. These discrepancies, they say, underestimate the actual value of investment, so much so that the real share of net investment in national income may be as high as 40 percent when using western methodology for calculating national income (Selunin 1988). Accordingly, CIA calculations of Soviet GNP by components (which are now the only available detailed estimates of Soviet GNP) show the share of investment in GNP in the 1970s and 1980s to exceed 30 percent for most years (Joint Economic Committee 1982, 1987; CIA/DIA 1989).

The same results may be obtained by calculating the share of consumption in Soviet national income and GNP, estimating then the share of investment as a residual. The share of basic types of personal income (for example, wages and salaries, pensions, stipends, and income of collective farmers) after necessary corrections—taxes, savings, subsidies—is around 60 percent of official national income, or less than 50 percent of national income, calcu-

2. In 1987, Soviet GNP originating from all industries (825 billion rubles) was 25 percent higher than GNP originating from material production (668 billion rubles). The proportion between total employment and employment in the sphere of material production is roughly the same (employment in service industries is 25-30 percent of total employment). Therefore, it can be estimated that Soviet national income, calculated according to western methodology, is 25-30 percent higher (roughly 700-750 billion rubles) than national income reported by official statistics.

3. OECD, Quarterly National Accounts, Table 1.

Table 3-1. Soviet National Income, GNP, and Investment
(Billions of Rubles, Current Prices)

	1980	1985	1986	1987	1988
National Income, Used for Consumption and Investment	454.1	568.7	546.0	585.8	613.7
Consumption	345.5	418.4	427.6	441.9	464.2
Personal Consumption	297.9	356.9	363.3	373.5	393.0
Cost of Materials and Supplies Consumed in Serv Industries	47.8	61.5	64.0	68.4	48.2
Accumulation	108.6	150.3	148.4	143.9	149.5
Change in Fixed Productive Capital Stock	45.5	46.1	50.4	53.5	45.5
Change in Fixed Unproductive Capital Stock	23.9	34.1	36.6	40.6	44.0
Change in Inventories and Reserves	39.2	70.1	61.4	49.8	63.9
Gross National Product	619.0	777.0	799.0	825.0	875.0
Gross Fixed Capital Investment	150.0	179.5	194.4	205.4[a]	218.2
Gross Fixed Nonresidential Capital Investment	129.8	151.4	163.5	171.9	182.6
Share of Accumulation in National Income (%)	23.9	26.4	25.8	24.6	24.0
Share of Gross Fixed Capital Investment in GNP (%)	24.4	23.1	24.3	24.9	24.9
Share of Gross Fixed Nonresidential Capital Investment in GNP (%)	21.0	15.5	20.5	20.8	20.9

a. In 1984 prices.

Source: Narodnoye Khozyaystvo SSSR, various years.

lated according to the western methodology.[4]   Therefore, if military expenditure accounts for 77 billion rubles, about 10 percent of national income originating in all industries, as was recently announced,[5] net investment may absorb as much as 40 percent of national income.   Many economists still believe that defense expenditure accounts for about 20 percent of national income (which falls in line with the CIA estimate of 15-17 percent of GNP), while the investments account for the other 30 percent. Thus, although the efficiency of these investments, as measured by growth rates of real GNP, is very low, it turns out that the Soviet Union spends an extremely large share of its national income and GNP on investment, a share at least as high as Japan, and probably much higher than in other western countries.

What are the reasons for such an exaggerated share of investment in Soviet national income and GNP, and for such an abnormally high capital/output ratio?   And what are the real requirements of the Soviet economy in investment funds currently and in the near future?   The obvious answer lies in the inefficiency of the so-called directive planning system, which is based on setting the enterprises' production quotas in physical terms and on the rationing of all supplies.   This system inevitably creates numerous disproportions, as it is impossible to envisage everything from above, to match the supply and demand for all the variety of products, to produce and deliver the proper product in the right place at the right time. Due to such factors, the capacity utilization rate in Soviet industries is extremely low: while official statistics put it at nearly 90 percent, independent estimates suggest that one-third of total fixed capital stands idle because of the "lack" of labor force.

Due to low efficiency of the system of rationed supply, extremely high inventories are needed for a nonstop work process.   In fact, inventories in the Soviet economy are almost as large as national income, while in the United States they are only approximately 30 percent of national income.   The inventory-to-sales ratio is 2.4 in the Soviet industrial sector and 3.6 in wholesale and retail trade. In the United States, the same ratios, even in the midst of a deep recession, do not exceed 1.9 and 1.7, respectively.   In the first half

4. *Moscow News*, No. 34, 1988.
5. *Pravda,* June 11, 1989.

of the 1980s, the Soviet Union spent an average of 6 percent of its annual national income to build up its inventories, while the United States spent less than 1 percent (Shmelev and Popov 1989).

There is another way to look at these figures. Viewed more positively, the large proportion of investment in Soviet national income is not only an indicator of inefficiency, but it can serve also as a reserve that could be used to increase consumption and accelerate economic growth. Combined with cuts in military expenditures, which are already being carried out, this could enable consumption to increase by nearly 50 percent without any additional increases in national income or existing capital and human stock, and without the improvement of current technology. Better organization and management of these resources could lead to increases in consumption without any additional inputs. In other words, if economic perestroika succeeds, and if losses in the form of excess investment in fixed capital stock and inventories are eliminated, there will be no need for such extensive investment, and the demand for capital will subsequently abate. Still, it would be wrong to draw from this conclusion that the overall demand for capital is going to shrink, as there are other requirements for additional funds.

II. THE NEED FOR ADDITIONAL FUNDS

The requirement for additional funds is associated primarily with the needs to eliminate the government budget deficit, to implement a pronounced social policy to meet the costs resulting from economic restructuring, to increase the expenditure for education and health care, and to replace obsolete and worn equipment in some industries.

Reducing the Government Budget Deficit

One cannot expect the market system to be efficient in the presence of the distortion in national monetary circulation that has occurred in recent years due to the accelerated growth of the money supply. The government budget deficit increased from an average of 20 billion rubles in the first half of the 1980s to 120 billion rubles in 1988, and is currently about 14 percent of GNP. The same average indicator for all OECD countries is less than 4 percent of GNP, and it is less than 3 percent in the United States. The problem is exacerbated by the fact that the deficit in the Soviet Union is financed not by government borrowing in financial markets, but mainly by printing money. Consequently, the gap between the amount of spendable money and the supply of goods is constantly increasing. In a system with fixed prices set by planning bodies, this gap largely manifests itself in increased shortages, as the increasing gap between the money demand for goods and the supply of those goods is not matched by increasing prices. Thus, it makes sense to speak about the rate of devaluation (or loss in purchasing power) of the ruble as resulting not only from inflation, but also from increased shortages.

The official consumer price index increases at a slow rate in the Soviet Union, registering a 1-percent annual increase in retail prices before 1989, and a 2-percent increase in 1989. However, such figures are questionable, as unofficial estimates for 1989 are 5-6 percent. In addition, shortages of goods are increasing even more quickly, so that the ruble may be losing purchasing power at a rate of 10-15 percent annually. This rate of currency devaluation is probably at a critical level; beyond this level, people try to rid themselves of unstable paper money, and a cumulative devaluation process develops, which increases the velocity of circulation and thus feeds inflation. This cumulative process distorts monetary circulation and makes it impossible for the government to use regulatory instruments effectively. The government can, in fact, lose control over the economic situation as its room to maneuver narrows. Therefore, it is absolutely crucial not only to considerably reduce the government budget deficit, but also to switch from deficit to surplus to pump out the excess money from circulation, thus liquidating accumulated monetary overhang and subsequently creating a healthy monetary environment for ongoing economic reforms.

An approved budget project for 1990 calls for reduction of the government budget deficit from over 90 billion rubles in 1989 to 60 billion rubles this year, as well as for reduction of cash-money emission from 18 billion rubles in 1989 to 10 billion rubles in

1990.[6] These are no doubt steps in the right direction, but they are clearly not enough. The personal accumulated delayed demand totaled 165 billion rubles at the beginning of 1990, that is, 40 percent of total retail sales of consumer goods and services (up from 20 percent in 1985).[7] Under such circumstances, the government should have planned the extraction of excess money out of circulation, not just the slowing down of the pace of money emission.

Increasing Social Security Expenditure

The Soviet Union is currently unprepared to deal with the problems that inevitably will be created by the move to a market economy. The transition will entail a substantial reallocation of resources. For example, many enterprises will be created and many will shut down, and millions of workers will have to change jobs. The distribution of income will become more uneven. Inflation and changes in relative prices may seriously affect the well-being of everyone, especially those on fixed incomes.

The present social security network can be regarded as obsolete, and it is unlikely able to withstand the pressures that would arise from the move to a market system. Unless there is a radical shift in the social welfare system—employee retraining, the old-age pension system, unemployment insurance, indexation of income, and the like—the transition to a market system may be accompanied by unacceptable damage to certain segments of Soviet society. Needless to say, this radical shift in social policy requires increased expenditure for social programs.

Increasing Expenditures for Education and Health Care

Investment in human capital, an essential ingredient of economic growth, is probably more important than investment in physical capital. Nevertheless, we are far behind major western countries. In the 1950s, we spent 10 percent of national income on education,

6. *Izvestiya,* August 5, 1989, and September 26, 1989.
7. *Izvestiya,* January 28, 1990.

which was more than most countries in the world at that time. However, subsequently, and in contrast to what occurred in other developed countries, education investment in the Soviet Union declined to its present 7 percent of national income, compared to 12 percent in the United States. Of 135,000 Soviet schools, just 9,000 (7 percent) have one computer-equipped classroom. Plans to increase the production of computers for classroom use are consistently not met; in the last three years, just 63,000 personal computers for classroom use (60 percent of the planned target) were produced.[8] If production continues to grow at the same pace, there is no hope that all schools will be equipped with computers before the turn of the century. It makes sense to find the funds to finance increased production or imports of personal computers now, so that at least in ten years those who enter the labor force will be properly trained.

Health care spending is less than 4 percent of Soviet national income, which is less than in all developed countries. In fact, more than 60 countries spend a greater portion of their national income for health care than we do. And though the economic benefits of expenditure for health are not as large as they are for investment in human capital, humanitarian concerns create an apparent need for increased spending in this area. The spread of AIDS, which has surfaced in some Soviet cities due to lack of disposable syringes, is a tragic example.

Increasing Investment in Replacement of Worn Equipment

One of the paradoxes of the system of directive planning is that over-investment in general coexists with under-investment in particular areas. The ratio of cumulative depreciation to gross value of fixed capital stock increased in the industrial sector from 26 percent in 1970 to 30 percent in 1975, 36 percent in 1980, and 46 percent in 1988.[9] The equipment is so old in some industries that it is dangerous to use: railways, electric power stations, and steel plants are currently using equipment that is completely worn and should have been retired long ago.

8. *Pravda,* May 13, 1989.
9. *Narodnoye Khozyaystvo SSSR,* various years; *Pravda,* May 24, 1989.

Fixed capital retirement is very slow in Soviet industry. The retirement ratio in the 1980s has been about 2 percent, compared to 4-5 percent in U.S. manufacturing. Moreover, more than 75 percent of all productive investment, compared to less than 50 percent in U.S. manufacturing, goes for the expansion of the existing capital stock, not for the replacement of retiring equipment and structures.

The depreciation rate for machinery and equipment in the industrial sector is on average 7-8 percent. It is assumed that the service life should be about 14 years, when, in fact, the average service life of equipment is now nearly two times longer at 27 years. One-third of all industrial equipment has already served more than ten years, 11 percent more than 20 years. In the petrochemical industry, nearly one-third of all equipment is older than its service life, in the auto industry, about 20 percent.[10]

So, while it is certainly true that the Soviet economy generally suffers from over-investment, there is also a need for a major restructuring of investment, associated in some areas and industries with considerable increases of capital investment, especially of investment in replacement of obsolete capital stock.

III. POSSIBLE OPTIONS TO MEET THE DEMAND FOR FUNDS

The aggregate demand for funds needed to balance the budget and to increase the outlays for the social security system, education, health care, and capital investment in some areas is estimated at up to 200 billion rubles per year, which is the equivalent of more than 20 percent of GNP or equal to all fixed capital investment in the Soviet economy. Where will these funds come from? The options are outlined below.

Cuts in Investment

Provided there is a huge over-investment in the Soviet economy, this would seem the most logical way to go. However, it is not. Some long-term investment projects that are likely to cause dam-

10. *Izvestiya*, September 23, 1989; Shmelev and Popov (1989, 146).

age (for example, diverting the northern rivers' flow), or those that would not begin to pay off until some time in the 21st century, surely should be cancelled. But at the same time, cuts in other investment areas are dangerous, as they may create even greater disproportions in an already unbalanced and severely strained economy. Shortages of materials and supplies for consumer goods production may become even more pronounced, and more bottlenecks in the economy may emerge.

The reduction in relative size of investment must and will be the natural consequence of a transition to a market economy. The reduction will occur because the market mechanism will be more efficient as far as resource allocation is concerned, that is, because utilization of production capacities will improve and the supply system will work without excess stockpiling of inventories. However, it will not be wise to speed up the event by administrative orders and commands *before the market mechanism starts to operate.* In the absence of the properly functioning market mechanism, all attempts to restructure the economy through mandatory reduction of the share of investment in favor of consumption may result in a disequilibrium, which could lead to depression.

Unfortunately, this may be a real possibility in 1990, as a draft plan worked out by the government, and approved by the Congress of People's Deputies, envisages the followings: (1) reduction of centralized government investment in material production by 25 percent; (2) cuts in imports of some investment goods; and (3) reduction of the share of investment in material production from 16 to 14 percent of national income. This implies that more than 1 million construction workers will have to change their jobs and/or occupations, moving from industrial construction to residential construction and the consumer goods industries. It is planned that because of this structural shift, the production of investment goods will increase by just 0.5 percent, while the production of consumer goods will increase by a healthy 6.7 percent.

Yet many observers consider these plans unrealistic because the general trend was the opposite in the past 60 years: the production of investment goods was growing much faster than that of consumer goods, so that the share of the latter in total industrial output

fell from 60 percent in 1928 to 25 percent in 1988.[11] There is a belief that without a transition to an efficient market economy, there
is, no way to ensure the increase of the share of consumption in
Soviet national income.

Increase of Consumer Goods Prices

Food prices—mostly for meat and milk products—are heavily
subsidized in the Soviet Union. The government could save up to
100 billion rubles if these subsidies were eliminated, leading to a
corresponding increase in prices. The issue has been widely
discussed since the very beginning of perestroika, but the
discussion has revealed that virtually everyone is against price
increases, even if they would be accompanied by direct money
compensation.

This opposition led the government to promise in the beginning of 1989 that prices for basic consumer goods would remain
unchanged in the course of the next two to three years. In fact, in
November 1989, President Gorbachev went as far as saying that an
unregulated market, if allowed, "in two weeks will force the people to get into the streets and will wipe out any government."[12]
This was clearly a reference to the possibility of deregulation of
prices for basic consumer goods.

Although the majority of academic economists is against consumer price increases, there are some (Soviet supply-siders) who favor immediate deregulation of all prices, including basic consumer
goods. In the fall of 1989, the All-Union Supreme Soviet voted
against proposed price increases for cigarettes, alcoholic beverages,
and some consumer luxury goods, though the Estonian parliament
did approve such increases.

Monetary Reform

This is another issue widely discussed in the Soviet Union. The
proposal is to exchange old money for new in the way it was done

11. *Narodnoye Khozyaystvo SSSR,* various years.
12. *Pravda,* November 6, 1989.

in the Soviet Union in 1947, or in West Germany in 1948: up to a certain amount at a ratio of 1:1, and after that at a ratio of 1:10, or, alternatively, also at a ratio of 1:1, provided that an individual prove that his or her money was earned legally.

The monetary reform was advocated until recently by extreme right-wingers, who claim that perestroika is leading to a restoration of capitalism, that the Mafia and the underground economy are gaining power, and that the cooperative sector is producing new Soviet millionaires linked to illegal activity. In December 1989, however, Gavril Popov and Boris Yeltsin—two leaders of the interregional group of deputies, which occupies the left side of the political spectrum—gave their support to the idea of monetary reform.

Advocates of monetary reform claim that 99 percent of the population supports the idea. Although there have been no public opinion polls conducted, the figure may be quite close to reality. (It may be of interest to note that a right-wing economist from the High School of Trade Union Movement, A. Sergeev, recently accused Yeltsin and Popov of stealing the idea, which he claims is incompatible with the leftist program and panders to the masses, from the right.)[13]

Yet most radical economists strongly oppose the monetary reform. They point out that the costs of the reforms will clearly outweigh the advantages. Recently published data on savings distribution reveal that of the 300 billion rubles of demand and saving deposits in the Saving Bank, those accounts that exceed 10,000 rubles total only to 30 billion rubles (and are probably owned by about 10 million families).[14] In short, the government will gain just 30 billion rubles—only 30 percent of the government budget deficit in 1989—if it decides to confiscate all savings in excess of 10,000 rubles (roughly equivalent to the price of a car). In doing so, the leadership will surely lose the confidence of the Soviet middle class, which is very socially active and has been the driving force behind perestroika. The confidence of the middle class, as well as the universal belief that property rights should never be violated, is worth much more than 30 billion rubles.

13. *Literaturnaya Rossiya,* February 12, 1990.
14. *Economicheskaya Gazeta,* No. 31, 1989.

Increase in Government Domestic Borrowing

An increase in government domestic borrowing may look like a positive development, as the value of government bonds held by individuals is negligible (25 billion rubles), and enterprises, cooperatives, and organizations do not hold government bonds at all. An increase may help ease the monetary overhang and transfer forced savings into voluntary savings (provided that the interest rate offered is relatively high, so as to protect investors from ruble devaluation). But measures stimulating internal borrowing have definite shortcomings: they do not affect the balance between savings and investment, and they can only contribute to assure the transition from forced savings to voluntary savings (which is somewhat helpful, but not enough).

In 1990, the government is going to offer to individuals 5-percent bonds totaling 15 billion rubles, and so-called "commodity bonds" (giving the right to buy goods in shortage) for 10 billion rubles. The government will also offer 5-percent bonds totaling 60 billion rubles to enterprises, co-ops, organizations, and banks. This will still leave the government with the need to print 10 billion rubles of new money, which is nonetheless down from 18 billion in 1989. There are also fears that money emission will actually be greater than expected because the interest rate offered to companies and individuals is not attractive enough for them to buy bonds.

Selling and Leasing Government Tangible Assets to Enterprises, Co-ops, and Individuals

This option looks promising for the following reasons: (1) state property is abundant; (2) there are many individuals and companies willing to buy or rent it; and (3) there will evidently be more such requests as market relations are developed. The constraint is, however, that it seems unlikely that the Supreme Soviet is going to allow private ownership of land and means of production. Until now, the government allowed work collectives and co-ops to buy and rent means of production, and private individuals to buy apartments, but it is still prohibited for individuals to buy equipment and structures for large-scale production operations (larger than a family business).

Increase in External Borrowing

This is the preferable way to go. Soviet gross international hard currency indebtedness by 1989 is estimated to be US$40-50 billion, and its net international indebtedness to be around US$30 billion; the debt-service ratio equals roughly 20-25 percent. Additionally, the Soviet Union has credits in rubles to socialist and developing countries of around US$60-65 billion.[15] Although these figures sharply contrast with recently published Soviet data (which claim 34 billion rubles debt in hard currency and a debt-service ratio of up to 75 percent), they are widely accepted by western experts.[16] The predominant view, in any case, is that the Soviet Union can double its hard currency debt without exposing itself to any serious risk. In addition, there is the possibility of using gold reserves, which are estimated at US$30 billion, as collateral for foreign credits. And increased foreign borrowing, coupled with the radical economic reform, may help considerably to meet transition costs without a decline in living standards.

It may be useful to examine current needs for foreign borrowing in the framework of savings and investment balance, which are presented in Table 3-2. While the balance is approximate because some crucial data are not published officially, the data still allow us to form a general impression of the relative size of funds needed to meet some urgent economic requirements.

15. *New York Times*, "The Soviet Economy in 1988: Gorbachev Changes Course," July 31, 1989, p. 44; *Financial Market Trends*, February 1989, p. 24-30.

16. *Izvestiya*, June 20, 1989. Soviet commentators believe that a very high debt-service ratio, reported by Nikolai Ryzhkov, may be explained if one takes into account short-term credits. In addition, it was announced recently that the official figure for total international indebtedness—34 billion rubles—includes the indebtedness to socialist countries in transferable rubles (3.6 billion rubles) and the debt in clearing arrangements with Yugoslavia and Finland (1.6 billion rubles), while the debt in hard currency equals 28.1 billion rubles (*Pravytelstvennyi Vestnik*, No. 9, 1989). The latest figure—a bit more than US$40 billion—approximately falls in line with western estimates of Soviet gross indebtedness in hard currency.

Table 3-2. Savings and Investment in the Soviet Economy in 1987
(Billions of Rubles, Current Prices)

	Estimate
Business Savings	150-160
Depreciation	72
Undistributed Profits of Enterprises and Collective Farms[a]	80-90
Personal Savings	26
Increase in Personal Deposits in Saving Banks	24
Government Bonds Sold to Individuals	2
Total, Gross Savings	180
Government Budget Deficit[b]	120
Government Revenues from Foreign Economic Operations[c]	84
Gross Nongovernment Domestic Investment	90
Noncentralized Investment of Government Enterprises[b, d]	72
Investment of Collective Farms[e]	15
Personal (Private) Investment for Residential Construction[e]	3
Change in Inventories[f]	-1

a. Estimate. Profits after taxes of government enterprises and collective farms minus payments to workers from profits and payment of interest rates on debt.

b. In 1988.

c. Planned target for 1990.

d. There is also so-called "centralized government investment" (114 billion rubles), which is financed directly from the government budget and thus is not included here.

e. In 1984 prices.

f. The figure does not correspond to the indicator from Table 3-1, "Change in Inventories and Reserves," which accounts for 50 billion rubles.

Sources: Narodnoye Khozyaystvo SSSR, various years; *Pravda,* October 28, 1989; *Izvestiya,* January 21, 1989; *Izvestiya,* September 26, 1989.

At first glance, the type of savings-investment balance in the Soviet Union resembles that in the United States, with the enormous government budget deficit absorbing half of all nongovernment domestic savings (business and personal). The difference, though, is that domestic savings are so large (due to the high level of undistributed profits) that most domestic nongovernmental investment can be financed without a large current account deficit (that is, without large capital inflow from abroad). Strictly speaking, the current account deficit, largely reflected in the data for government revenues from foreign trade, arises mainly from the differences in domestic prices (as compared to world prices) of exported and imported goods. Exports, consisting primarily of raw materials, are low-priced, while imports, consisting primarily of manufactured goods, are high-priced. When such inequities are corrected by pric' changes or the establishment of reasonable import duties, a significant portion of the foreign trade deficit will disappear,[17] leaving room to increase the foreign trade deficit, financing it by the inflow of foreign capital.

If the Soviet Union is to increase imports of consumer goods using borrowing abroad, then real consumption will increase at the expense of previously forced savings, which will decrease. Nevertheless, there will be no need to cut investments, as they may be financed from increased government revenues from sales of imported goods. Thus, it is possible to kill two birds with one stone: (1) eliminate forced savings, which are currently causing much distress and allowing increased real consumption, and (2) avoid forced cuts in investment by financing them through increased revenues from sales of imported goods.

Without radical market-type reforms, foreign borrowing may provide only temporary relief, while aggravating the situation in the long run: in five to seven years, the country will end up with a balance-of-payments crisis, a lack of hard currency to repay the debt, and a lack of an efficient market economy that will be able to generate higher real incomes, thus making it necessary to cut consumption to repay the debt. In other words, foreign borrowing

---

17. The government budget deficit in this case will remain unchanged, as the reduction of government revenues from external economic operations will be counterweighted by the reduction of government outlays to subsidize low raw material prices or by increased government revenues from tariff duties.

is the preferable way of financing the costs of transition to an efficient market economy. If radical reforms to assure this transition are not implemented, increased borrowing will be destructive in the longer run.

REFERENCES

Abalkin, L. 1989. "Nuzchna Programma Ozdorovleniya." *Moskovskiye Novosty,* February 5.
Aganbegyan, A. 1989. "Gde Naity Milliardy?" *Izvestiya,* August 1.
Antonov, M. 1989. "Vyhod Yest." *Nash Sovremennyk,* No. 8.
CIA/DIA. 1989. "The Soviet Economy in 1988: Gorbachev Changes Course." A paper presented by the CIA and DIA to the National Security Economic Subcommittee of the Joint Economic Committee, U.S. Congress, April 12, p. 38-40.
Joint Economic Committee. 1982. "U.S.S.R.: Measures of Economic Growth and Development, 1950-1980." Studies prepared for the use of the Joint Economic Committee, U.S. Congress, p. 76-78.
———. 1987. "Gorbachev's Economic Plans, Vol. 1." Study papers submitted to the Joint Economic Committee, U.S. Congress.
Kosolopov, R. 1989. "Vse Tot Zche Vopros: Chto Delat?" *Economicheskiye Nauki,* No. 8.
Latsis, O. 1989. ". . . I Kak Nam Stat Bogache." *Izvestiya,* May 10.
McKinnon, R. 1989. *The Order of Liberalization for Opening the Soviet Economy.* Stanford, CA: Stanford University.
Selunin, V. 1988. "Tempi Rosta Na Vesakh Petreblenia." *Sotcialisticheskaya Industriya,* January 5.
Shatalyn, S. 1989. "Ne Gadaem na Kofeinoi Gusche." *Pravda,* February 18.
Shmelev, N. 1989. Presentation at the Congress of People's Deputies. *Izvestiya,* June 9.
Shmelev, N., and V. Popov. 1989. *The Turning Point: Revitalizing the Soviet Economy.* New York: Doubleday, pp. 133-34.

_____

CHAPTER 4

Perestroika: The Demand for Capital

ALEXEI KUNITSIN

Examining possible forms and sources of investment in the Soviet economy today requires analysis of the nation's social and economic problems and the steps being taken by the Soviet government to improve the situation. Perestroika has entered a critical phase. Soviet society lacks the economic reform to accompany the spiritual and political liberalization. Unless tangible results are achieved in the very near future, the situation in various parts of the Soviet Union threatens to get out of control and may have grave consequences. The increasing number of strikes and political, ideological, and ethnic conflicts suggest that this process is already under way. Top priority must be given to supplying the domestic market with consumer goods, foodstuffs, household appliances, housing, and medical services.

The Soviet government has responded to this crisis with a package of emergency measures that form the basis of the drafted state economic and social development plan for 1990. Taken together, these measures call for an unprecedentedly large rechanneling of resources to satisfy the demand for consumer goods and services. This paper examines the positive and negative effects the proposed measures might have on the Soviet economy, and its prospects for interaction with the foreign business community.

SHORT-TERM FORECAST

The potential success of the emergency measures is severely hampered, because at the beginning of 1989, the state's domestic debt was 312 billion rubles; the budget deficit was 120 billion rubles (14 percent of GNP); and Soviet foreign debt stood at 34 billion rubles (US$54 billion at the official exchange rate). Attempts to hold it back thus far have been futile. To make matters worse, nominal personal income growth has been nearly twice that of consumer goods production.

The drafted 1990 plan aims first to reduce critical economic shortages and remove the causes of social tension. Second, as a plan that precedes the 13th five-year period (1991-1995), it seeks to establish the basis for steady, near-term development of the Soviet economy. The government believes that simultaneously hitting these targets requires emergency decisionmaking.

A 12-percent jump in consumer goods production is planned, and total GNP growth is targeted at 2 percent. Retail trade must grow by 40 billion rubles, compared to an annual average increase of 15 billion rubles in the past four years. A one-third reduction in centralized capital investment together with a sharp decrease in industrial construction is planned in the production sphere to invigorate the economy. State budget allocations will be cut even more in a number of industries, including the metallurgy, fuel, and energy industries, which will experience a 40-percent cut in their budget allocations.

A sharp decrease in imports of certain goods and equipment, primarily those used for heavy industry, will cause production cuts in some sectors. For example, lower cold-rolled sheet metal imports means an absolute reduction in the output of trucks and other equipment. Hard currency thus saved will be used for the purchase of up to 10 billion rubles of consumer goods at retail prices.

Reaction

Will the Soviet economy withstand such a dramatic and comprehensive structural redistribution? Can the 1990 plan be perilous for the tense strings of the industrial production mechanism?

The planners are focusing primarily on two important reserves: conversion of military production to civilian uses, and acceleration of the economic reform. Defense sector enterprises are expected to raise their 1990 consumer goods output 1.4-fold. The General Staff of the Soviet Armed Forces predicts that their enterprises can produce 250-270 billion rubles worth of consumer goods between 1991 and 1995. Doing so will raise the share of civilian products by more than 60 percent by 1995, by which time annual output of consumer goods must grow by nearly 50 billion rubles, or 10-12 percent of all retail trade, and a nearly one-third increase from the present level of total consumer goods trade.

A deepening and more radical economic reform is expected to achieve the most significant results, however. Some improvements have already been achieved. Industrial enterprises grew from 1,000 in 1988 to 2,748 by July 1989, operating on the second form of the self-accounting model. Sixty collective producers in industry leased their enterprises by October 1, 1988; 638 did so as of April 1, 1989; and by July 1, 1989, there were 903 such firms. An additional 1,100 enterprises in other branches were using innovative forms of management by 1989.

Prospects for Success

As planned, extensive conversion and intensive economic reform will generate a dramatic acceleration of consumer goods production. How realistic are these plans and what can their consequences be?

There is little doubt about reaching these goals in terms of money value, but an actual "great leap" in the production of consumer goods appears to be unlikely. According to the 1990 plan, television production, which grew by 257,000 sets over the previous three years, is to increase to 835,000 sets; washing machine output is to grow by 1.6 million to a total of 2.6 million units; output of vacuum cleaners is to increase by 2.2 million, after growing by only 730,000 in the previous three years; VCR output is to increase by 3.7 times; and a 300-percent increase in mini-tractors is also projected.

The defense sector enterprises can hardly provide such growth. Retooling for manufacturing household appliances can take at least 18 to 24 months. New equipment has to be manufactured and installed, the work force has to be retrained, suppliers of spare parts and components have to be found (who, in turn, must have their

own production facilities ready and suppliers secured), and, last but
not least, the latter must be prepared to market their products and
handle post-sale maintenance.

It would hardly be wise to overestimate the capabilities of producers in the military sector. First, their supplies and materials
are, as a rule, too costly for civilian production. On the one hand,
high production costs will restrain the growth of production; on
the other, they will stimulate the growth of domestic market
prices, which would prevent them from reaching their goal of
making the consumer goods market a balanced one. Second, with
a greater share of civilian product in their output, the military
enterprises will be losing their priority supply status. Also, the
existing outflow of work force to cooperatives cannot be neglected.

It is not yet time to flatter ourselves about the development of
new forms of management. Statisticians say that the second form
of self-accounting, which is far from perfect, is used by only 6 percent of industrial enterprises. Real Soviet economic reform
achievements are much more modest because local party leaders
and top managerial officials are at times too rushed to report their
victories to Moscow. These achievements quite often involve only
some formal alterations. It is highly unlikely that 3-5 percent (or
even 10-15 percent) of all industrial enterprises could dramatically
change the current economic situation. Changes are pressing, but
no one is saying the administer-and-command system is not viable. A drastic rise in consumer goods production will, it seems,
run parallel to the genuine massive transfer by Soviet manufacturers to progressive managerial methods, which can become an obstacle to reaching the goals planned for 1990.

A decree of the Supreme Soviet, "On Taxation of the Wages Fund
of State Enterprises," which became valid on October 1, 1989, also
has implications for the planned structural shift. The decree has
been adopted as an anti-inflationary measure. It introduces a progressive scale for taxing the incremental enterprise funds used for
payment of wages (see Table 4-1). The consumer goods production
sphere is exempt from the provisions of the new regulation. On
the one hand, the new regulation will undoubtedly stimulate the
growth of consumer goods production and services, and it will
make it possible to use those in the work force more efficiently by

Table 4-1. Scale of Rates of the Regulating Taxes
on the Increment of Wage-Payment Funds

Percent	Taxes Paid to the State Budget (Rubles per each Ruble in the Increment Wage Fund)
Below 3	None
3 to 5	1
5 to 7	2
Over 7	3

reducing their number and increasing the wages of those who remain. It must be exactly these results that motivated lawmakers to prepare the new decree.

However, consequences of a different nature are also possible. A large number of Soviet manufacturers that produce some specialized goods have very limited choices in applying their technologies. An overwhelming majority of enterprises is short of skilled personnel and may be forced to raise prices. Indeed, with the officially acknowledged inflation rate of 8 percent (it is actually higher), wage increases of 3 percent in sectors exempt from taxation still mean losses of workers' real income of 5 percent. Managers who find themselves unable to compensate for inflation run the risk of losing skilled personnel, who might join a cooperative or leave for more inventive managers. This staff drain is a reality now, with about 3 million personnel lost in 1988.

In the long run, the new taxation regulation will hold back inflation in some spheres, even while raising it in others. Despite an abundance of restrictions, Soviet managers fully understand and have mastered the correct strategy for dealing with implicit inflation. To compensate for an 8-percent money devaluation, wage funds must be raised by at least 32 percent (8 percent of which goes to the worker and 24 percent of which is tax payment to the state budget—see Table 4-1). Therefore, the power of the state to force a wage freeze is in reality very limited because it risks a fast withdrawal of the work force from producing machines and equipment, which in turn can shatter the economy's already quite unreliable intermediate goods sector.

The latter consideration deserves elaboration. It is inescapable that the vital increase in consumer goods production must be accomplished within the framework of the infamous and ineffective administrative-and-command system, and mainly at the expense of simple resource redistribution. Such redistribution is risky because the situation is already critical in primary production and heavy industries, such as metallurgy, chemicals, and machine building. This is evidenced by the slack discipline of contractual supplies and the growing disorganization of the Soviet economic mechanism.

On the surface, all looks fine. Industrial enterprises fulfilled 98.9 percent of their planned contractual supplies in 1988. Nonsupplied products amounted to 8.6 billion rubles (12.2 billion in 1987). In the first six months of 1989, contractual supplies were fulfilled, with a production lack of a "mere" 2.8 million rubles. The number of manufacturers that failed to meet their contractual obligations was 14 percent in 1988, compared to 17 percent in 1989. In the machine-building industry, the figure is 32 percent in 1988, compared to 40 percent in 1989.

These figures could be taken as good news if they were not absolutely unrealistic. Management agencies and the mass media are absolutely overwhelmed by a storm of complaints about failures to obtain supplies on time and erratically available supplies of spare parts and units. According to Deputy Chief State Arbitrator of the Russian Federation B. Puginsky:

> The existing system of registration of fulfillment of contracts is so inaccurate and has so many loopholes in it that it has turned into a lying mirror. Our economy cannot even recognize itself in it. The manufacturer can have his fulfillment report registered if he can start deliveries on the last day of the month, or for that matter, of the quarter. Violations of reporting dates are not registered, while every industry needs its resources daily. The norm in an industrialized society is not deliveries once a month, but strict observance of daily or even hourly schedules.
>
> The realistic picture is largely obscured by numerous "additions" to statistical reports. Every other manufacturer tries to fool the in

spector and lie to State officials. Despite the provision stipulating that costs of rejected or unserviceable goods will be subtracted from supply reports, they are safely there. Losses due to unserviceable production handling exceed 1 billion rubles a year. It has become quite usual for suppliers to replace items on the agreed-upon supplies list with different ones. Not infrequently are consumers being pressured to portray the supplies situation as normal.[1]

Quite a few enterprises continue to exist only due to their utter negligence of environmental protection requirements.

Aggravating this critical situation is the fact that more than half of all machines and equipment in Soviet factories are ten years old or older. Although the average age of Soviet equipment is not much greater than in the West, its inferior quality causes it to become outdated at a much quicker pace. The lack of specialized and especially precision equipment is also felt strongly.

While the share of equipment aged five years or less has grown considerably in the West during the past decade (from 26 to 30 percent in Great Britain, for example), the share of new equipment and machines in the Soviet Union has decreased from 46 percent in 1974, to 40 percent in 1980, and to 35 percent in 1985.[2] Production facilities that have been commissioned or retooled in the past two years have been operating at only 75 percent of capacity.

The existing economic system promotes deficits, which in the long run greatly affect the consumer. Of 1,200 staple goods monitored by experts in 140 cities and towns, only 200 are on sale comparatively steadily. Under these conditions, massive rechanneling of material resources and the work force from the primary goods sector to the consumer goods sectors can shortly provoke paralysis of our economy and further restrict its chances for solving social problems.

This very risky maneuvering with resources is justified by a desire to keep control over the economy. Speaking at a session of the Supreme Soviet, government spokesperson Yu Maslyakov pointed out, "We in the centralized governmental management level cannot at this stage let go of all the strings and levers of the

1. *Pravda,* August 27, 1989, p.1.
2. *Economic Survey of Europe in 1986-1987.* United Nations Economic Commission for Europe, New York, 1987, p. 165.

national economy."[3] While such a situation appears very unlikely
at present, there remains the stubborn desire to maintain the status
quo, even though the decision not to rock the boat—which is
sinking!—may result in quite a sorry situation.

It has never been more important to muster all the reserves
available, for which initiative and entrepreneurship must be un-
leashed, giving up all the senseless restrictions and regulations. It
is necessary to lower taxes. As for consequences, the economy
"overheating" with all its explosive character is less risky as a policy than its long overdue "underheating," which promises degra-
dation and even a break-up of heavy industry, the backbone of our
economy.

To conclude, it appears quite likely that during approximately
the next 18 months, the Soviet consumer goods market situation
will remain about the same. The list of consumer goods in shortage may become shorter, but goods will still be in short supply.
The social effect of the growth of production of consumer goods and
their purchases abroad will be diminished by inflationary processes and also will be spent on temporary settlement of regional
conflicts in various parts of the nation. Social tension is likely to
stay, and it may even become worse, which would accelerate the
break-up of the administer-and-command system, enabling Soviet
society to switch to the principles of a market economy.

PROBLEMS OF FOREIGN TRADE

To correctly evaluate prospects of western investment in the Soviet
economy, it is indispensable to examine the current foreign trade
situation. One of its most acute problems is growing debt. Then
there is the raw materials orientation of our trade with the West,
which becomes stronger every year. The need to import greater
quantities of foodstuffs, metals, and a wide scope of chemicals is
growing, and the imbalance of export and import activities is becoming greater, especially in transactions involving hard currency. The hardships we are experiencing now in foreign trade
and current account position are rooted in the deterioration of our

3. *Pravda,* August 5, 1989.

stock of machines and equipment. Another cause is ineffective management-level organization of production.

At present, some 25 million different goods and commodities are manufactured in the Soviet Union, many of which depend on our imports. The foreign trade sector of our economy amounts to a mere 7 percent of Soviet gross national product, which is approximately 2.5 times less than the world average. But even such a relatively low level of import dependence is quite important to our economy.

Machines and equipment imports, which equal less than 3-4 percent of those made locally, are the most important Soviet imports from developed capitalist countries. In contrast, the leading industrial countries import one-third to one-half of all the equipment they need.[4] The only exception in this category is Japan, which imports only 7 percent of its national equipment requirements.

Beyond its volume, the extent of import dependence is determined first and foremost by the function the imported equipment plays. Unique precision machines and equipment, electronic devices, and instruments imported from the West, which are used in key technological processes and operations, have a low share of the total volume of industrial production, but they are essential to achieving a competitive technological level for the manufactured product. In most cases, equipment manufactured in the Soviet Union or other socialist countries cannot be substituted for western machinery due to its relatively low quality and the production capacity constraints of the Soviet machinery and equipment enterprises. Thus, the comparatively low percentage of western equipment in the stock of machines in the Soviet Union often conceals a deep technological dependence on the West.

The cumulative effects of this dependence begin to be felt at the sub-branch level and by individual manufacturers after western equipment has been imported for some time. Those that import most of their equipment from developed capitalist countries, such as

---

4. For example, metal-cutting, forging, and pressing equipment. The share of imports in national consumption (production plus import minus export) amounts to: West Germany, 29 percent; Italy, 32 percent; the United States, 42 percent; France, 56 percent; Switzerland, 59 percent; Sweden, 67 percent; Austria, 107 percent; and Belgium, 133 percent.

the Soviet chemical industry, are increasingly dependent on imported western equipment. Available data indicate that nearly 30
percent of ethylene, almost 50 percent of benzene, 65 percent of
methanol and polysterol, and nearly 90 percent of polyethylene,
polypropylene, and a number of other synthetic fibers are being
produced in the Soviet Union using western equipment. This is
especially noteworthy in view of the fact that most high-technology
products are being produced on western equipment. And it is these
goods that play a pivotal role in the structure of the Soviet economy.
Given the interrelationship of modern manufacturing, these foreign goods are essential to both the actual production and rates of
technological progress in many branches of Soviet industry.

Such a situation offers no cause to be concerned as long as a country has reliable sources of hard currency incomes, as economic
interdependence is quite normal today. Even if any of our suppliers
opted for a boycott or sanctions, the hard currency would enable
individuals and enterprises to purchase readily available suitable
substitutes. Moreover, dependence on imports is quite healthy
because countries usually buy better and cheaper products abroad
than are available locally. Other things being equal, the more
foreign-made goods a country can import, the better off the
economy.

Unfortunately, many Soviet industries' imports from the West
do not rest on a solid foundation of a multitude of exportable manufactured goods. On the contrary, the import capacity of the Soviet
Union now is perched precariously on two quite unreliable
crutches: oil and natural gas exports. Fuels provide nearly half of
Soviet export earnings and, in its trade with the West, up to 80 percent of Soviet hard currency incomes.

Under these conditions, the Soviet economy has become a virtual
hostage of global fossil fuels market conditions and the mineral
fuels situation. The first alarm was sounded in 1985, when market
prices for oil fell 45 percent. The state treasury lost billions of
petrodollars, a loss that translates to 37 billion rubles in lost production for the entire economy over the past four years. Added to
lost hard currency export earnings in the world in 1988-1989, the
price of grain, a major import item, increased drastically. To
make matters even worse, Soviet agricultural output in 1988 was the
lowest in three years.

Faced with this situation, the state was forced to make general cuts in hard currency allocations, which left enterprises without western-made equipment, spare parts, raw materials, and components needed for trouble- and accident-free production.[5]

The vitally needed restoration of economic balance to satisfy industrial and consumer needs and dwindling hard currency export earnings are the central causes of the swelling external debt, which is already twice as much as the volume of the Soviet Union's hard currency exports and still growing. However, the main dangers associated with its minimal participation in the international division of labor still lie ahead for the Soviet economy. Technological progress is impossible without constantly expanding the scope of manufactured goods. Economists forecast a doubling of the number, and a significant increase in the sophistication of manufactured goods over the next 20 years, because the manufactured goods trade will grow absolutely and relative to production. Therefore, more extensive participation in the international division of labor is a prerequisite to future industrial development. Failure to do so promises only growing economic and technological backwardness.

No matter how diversified the Soviet Union's (or any other country's) economic system is, general import substitution, without lost real income, is impossible on both economic and technological grounds. Moreover, the acute shortage of state-of-the-art equipment and quality materials, and the lack of significant import substitution, will inevitably strip the corresponding fields of industry naked, causing a similar supply crisis, albeit elsewhere within the economy.

---

5. Partly, that is where one should look for the roots of the recently more frequent crashes and accidents in industrial enterprises and in the transportation system breaks in the supply of electric power, water, and other major and minor disturbances and emergencies. Without sufficient foreign currency to participate in the international division of labor at levels typical among developed capitalist countries, the Soviet Union tries to achieve the unachievable by attempting to produce everything with its own hands. And insufficient supplies of equipment, raw materials, and spare parts quite often force enterprises to use outdated technology, and thus to manufacture quite a lot of low-quality products that have to be used for various applications. The 1990 plan envisages a redistribution of considerable amounts of hard currency resources for the purchase of consumer goods abroad—and that may still aggravate the situation in the Soviet industry.

There is no choice. Increased imports, and a corresponding increase in hard currency earnings to pay for them, are essential to Soviet industrial development. Alternative uses of present-day hard currency earnings are very limited because any currently saved—for example, due to smaller grain purchases—must be directed toward lowering the Soviet external debt burden.

On the contrary, the Soviet Union's inability to earn enough hard currency could lead to very serious troubles. Any disturbance in exports and imports in the very near future could cause a chain reaction of shortages, more equipment downtime, lower total incomes, and temporary unemployment throughout the economy. Some sectors of the economy could be paralyzed if production disturbances become too severe.[6]

In sum, the difficulties now being experienced in the Soviet Union's domestic and foreign sectors have a common denominator: the unsatisfactory state of our manufacturing base, as is evidenced by more frequent supplies failures, heavier incidences of having too many goods in short supply, and the inevitable purchases of many types of consumer goods abroad. To overcome these difficulties and to make perestroika a success, we have to retool our production facilities as soon as possible. However, the planned transfer of large amounts of money into the consumer goods sector can seriously restrain this modernization and, given the slow-going economic reform, consequently can worsen the economic situation in the Soviet Union rather than improve it.

Perestroika and Western Business

Paradoxically, the worsening of our situation may lead to an intensive integration of the Soviet economy into the world economy and to a fast-growing interaction with western business. The main obstacle today is a set of administrative regulations and restrictions, both explicit and *de facto*, remaining in export and import sectors, and in hard currency and credit operations. Social and economic problems will make the government look for any available reserve

---

6. Although more remote, the simple continuation of the current oil and gas export dystrophy could have similar results.

promising to stimulate production growth. The most promising among these seems to be cooperation with firms of industrially developed countries.

The financial slant toward the consumer goods sector creates favorable opportunities for western producers of foodstuffs, clothing, footwear, medicines, detergents, and many more types of consumer goods that are in short supply on the Soviet market. Additional hard currency purchases may amount to US$1.5-2 billion. However, the consumer goods boom will go hand-in-hand with a rapidly rising demand for imported industrial products and equipment, various instruments, spare parts and components, and materials. Export hard currency earnings will be insufficient to cover both fields, so more action will be needed in the form of credits to attract foreign investment from individual entrepreneurs.

The main form of individual foreign investment will undoubtedly be joint ventures. As of September 1, 1989, there were nearly 800 of them registered in the Soviet Union, with foreign capital of about 1 billion rubles. In the past several months, joint ventures have been booming thanks to easier registration procedures, additional tax graces, and extension of rights of foreign partners. Legal, administrative, and other issues that previously inhibited foreign business representatives are being settled.

However, the main problems remain. The primary issue is safeguarding the ability of joint ventures to be self-accounting in terms of hard currency, that is, to provide for their purchases of the required commodities and services while securing the foreign partner's profit. This problem largely stems from the low competitiveness of Soviet industrial products and from outdated and worn-out equipment. In times when state-of-the-art equipment and quality materials are very much in demand on the domestic market, joint ventures must look for their suppliers in the West, a situation that adds another financial burden. The difficulties with material and technological supplies account for the fact that only one-third of all the registered joint ventures are operational. The overwhelming majority of them are in the services business, with only about 30 engaged in industrial production.

The difficult situation can be made easier with more active participation of the military production sector, which is now being converted to civilian production. The contribution of the Soviet part-

ners in joint ventures could become greater if currently unused results of research and development programs and inventions (their
number is several tens of thousands) are used. Holding hard currency auctions also seems promising, but despite the decision to
hold them, there have not been any. However, the only way to
overcome the hard currency barrier is to raise the competitiveness
of Soviet industrial production through a radical change in the
Soviet understanding of the term "property," retool industrial facilities, and pursue an aggressive export stimulation policy.

Free economic zones offer another way of attracting foreign capital technology and management skills to the Soviet Union. It has
already been decided to establish one of these at Vyborg, near
Leningrad close to the Soviet-Finnish border (a scientific and production zone), and in the Nakhodka area in the Far East, where
extensive processing of raw materials will be carried out. A tourist
and production zone is being actively worked out in Novgorod in
Central Russia. A similar project is being considered for Sochi, on
the Black Sea.

Legislation for free economic zones has yet to be worked out, but
as pilot projects these zones are being set up as autonomous self-
accounting units having their own budget and balance sheets.
They will be run by a special board accountable to local authorities.
Each board will represent the zone's manufacturers in their interaction with the state and bordering regions. The flow of goods
and services in and out of the zone and foreign countries will be
exempt from all taxes. There will be no tariff or licensing restrictions.

The primary goals in establishing these zones are stimulating
joint investment and entrepreneurial activities, attracting advanced western technology and managerial know-how to the Soviet
economy, and filling the domestic market with quality goods.
One must bear in mind, however, that the contribution of these
zones to solving the hard currency issue will not be meaningful before the second half of the 1990s. At least two or three years will be
necessary to prepare the territory, to build production, management, and residential buildings, and to develop the necessary infrastructure. It also takes time to settle legal, financial, and organizational problems.

Such factors require massive centralized allocations, including hard currency. Given the present balance-of-payments situation, the demand for hard currency may be satisfied to a great extent with the help of foreign credits. Therefore, even if in their first years free economic zones do have positive hard currency balances (which is highly unlikely, given the world economy's experience), the state will not receive extra hard currency returns, for they will go to creditors.

The chief implication is that a sharp increase in the Soviet Union's foreign debt can be expected in the near future. It can result from the shortage in hard currency earnings from our exports. The losses due to the drop of oil and gas prices (from 160 rubles a ton in 1985 to 60 rubles a ton in 1988) amounted to 25 billion rubles in convertible currency in the past three years alone, and compensating for them by increasing earnings through larger exports of manufactured goods has not been possible. At the same time, budget allocations in the consumer goods sector have grown. Some 31 billion rubles were spent on production of foodstuffs in 1986-1988. In 1989, imports of consumer goods and foodstuffs are expected to equal 22 billion rubles, including more than 5 billion rubles in convertible currency for the purchase of grain and foodstuffs alone.

The current lack of hard currency, which could be used for retooling old western equipment, purchasing spare parts and materials, and developing related production spheres, has sharply aggravated the instability of manufacturing operations and has led to breakdowns in planned supplies. Only new hard currency credits can stop, or at least hold back, this dangerous process.

Another reason for an expected growth of our foreign debt is its own inertia, which appears to get more and more out of the government's control. The demand for imports, combined with a limited ability to pay for them, has created a situation in which the Soviet Union's hard currency debt is twice as big as its annual income from goods and services exports. Servicing the debt requires drawing on short-term credits, which are becoming larger and larger. The Soviet economy does not even have enough oil and gas export earnings to pay the interest on the credits. The nation has stepped over its "red line" between repayment for credits and credits in hard currency. The inertia of debt self-growth continues, and the government has failed to find a way out of the situation.

Describing the growing difficulties is not, however, an attempt to state that business opportunities for western companies in the Soviet Union will become scarce. The opposite appears to be true. Every new development in the spiral of the economic crisis shatters the society in such a powerful way that people with initiative and energy come to the fore. There are now fresh and viable forces coming through the cracks in the monolithic structure of the administer-and-command system. There are cooperatives, working collectives that lease their enterprises, associations of manufacturers, societies of shareholders, business concerns, and commercial banks. They are experiencing severe struggle and terrible pain. The captains of our industrial enterprises are getting wiser. Workers can move more rapidly. Of course, the new economic forces cannot as yet offer million-dollar orders to western business leaders asking to build gigantic enterprises. They have not been able to get their share of Soviet petro- and gas-dollars. But they do constitute the future of the Soviet economy. The process of primary capital accumulation goes on, as Soviet people gain experience and develop international business connections. Our partners in the West who are concerned for the future rather than sulking over past supercontracts with those Soviets could think of new targets in their eastern strategies. The time is favorable now to sow on the Russian soil, which may soon yield a good crop.

Convertibility

A Phased Plan for Making the Ruble Convertible: A Multilateral Proposal

JOSEF C. BRADA, VLADIMIR POPOV,
MARIE LAVIGNE, ALEXANDER BELOV, SCOTT PARDEE,
ALEXANDER PARKANSKY and FRANCIS SCOTLAND

I. INTRODUCTION

A. The Inconvertibility of the Ruble

The ruble is currently inconvertible both for foreigners and for Soviet residents. Foreigners are not allowed to hold rubles or to freely convert the rubles they acquire into foreign currency (or vice versa). This form of inconvertibility is called external financial inconvertibility. Moreover, foreigners also face commodity inconvertibility, which means that, because most goods within the Soviet Union are allocated by the government, ruble holders are not permitted to purchase goods, particularly inputs and machinery, at any price without consent of the government. Soviet residents, both individuals and enterprises, also face such commodity inconvertibility, as well as internal financial inconvertibility. The latter means that they cannot freely exchange rubles into foreign currencies.

The inconvertibility of the ruble was consistent with the Soviet Union's centralized economic system and with the state's monopoly over foreign trade. All trade transactions with market

economies were denominated and paid in hard currencies that
were received or disbursed by the central bank. Decisions on trade
were made by planners, generally without reference to domestic
and foreign prices, a practice necessitated by the arbitrary nature of
Soviet prices. Enterprises and ministries seeking imported goods
competed for them not by their willingness to pay, but rather by
influencing those responsible for trade decisions. Nor did Soviet
producers seek foreign markets; rather, they provided goods for export when ordered to do so.

While such a system enabled Soviet planners to maintain the
control over the volume and commodity composition of trade required to implement the domestic economic plan, it had numerous
shortcomings: an inability to determine the volume and pattern of
trade most consistent with the Soviet Union's international competitiveness and comparative advantage; the failure to provide competition for Soviet producers on their own markets; and a tendency
toward an isolationist, inward-looking development of the Soviet
economy.

B. Convertibility and Perestroika

The negative consequences of ruble inconvertibility have not been
lost on Soviet leaders, nor has the incompatibility of an inconvertible ruble with a reform of the Soviet economy that seeks to decentralize decisionmaking on the basis of market signals. Indeed,
one can argue that the successful reform of the Soviet economy is a
prerequisite for making the ruble fully convertible. At the same
time, it is inconceivable that the obstacles to reform that exist in
the Soviet Union can be overcome without important contributions
from the foreign trade sector. Thus, ruble convertibility and the
success of perestroika are inextricably linked.

C. Specific Benefits of Ruble Convertibility

By achieving ruble convertibility, Soviet leaders wish to establish
an organic link with the world economy. In the current circumstances they hope to obtain the following benefits:

1. Increased efficiency in foreign trade, including an expansion of trade with the West; a change in the structure of foreign trade to assist in the restructuring of industry and to improve the Soviet Union's comparative advantage in manufactures; and greater imports of capital goods and technology. Imports will go to the most productive rather than the most persuasive enterprises, and exporters will have to meet world standards.

2. A more efficient domestic economy where producers will face competition from imports, thus providing an important stimulus to the drive for market responsiveness and higher quality. The speed and efficiency with which both foreign and domestic technology are acquired and disseminated will increase.

3. Ruble convertibility will encourage foreign investment in the Soviet Union, thus providing western technology and capital for the reconstruction of the Soviet economy. Currently, ruble inconvertibility severely limits the size and scope of the activities of Soviet-western joint ventures and effectively precludes other, more innovative forms of foreign participation in the Soviet economy. Ruble convertibility would both increase the confidence of western investors in the Soviet economy and greatly enhance their ability to participate in it.

D. Barriers to Convertibility

Despite the importance of convertibility to the success of perestroika, the obstacles to even a limited convertibility of the ruble are daunting. Among the most serious are:

1. Lack of a functioning domestic market and the resulting irrational price system. Prices in the Soviet Union are administratively set, and they reflect neither the need to balance supply and demand nor the true cost of production. Thus, the prices of some goods, such as food, fuels, and raw materials, are artificially low, while those of other goods are well above the cost of production. Trade based on such prices would be both irrational and harmful to Soviet firms and consumers.

2. Excess purchasing power in the Soviet economy represents a pent-up demand for foreign goods. Rather than permitting in-

creasing consumer prices to reflect the more rapid growth of wages and incomes than of the availability of consumer goods, the Soviets have resorted to formal and informal rationing to allocate these goods. This has forced consumers to acquire large hoards of rubles that represent undesired savings awaiting an outlet. If the ruble were made convertible for Soviet firms and citizens, the result would be a massive buying spree for foreign goods that would far exceed the Soviet Union's ability to earn foreign exchange.

3. A desire to protect the population from negative economic consequences of convertibility. Trade with the West on a more open basis will lead to dislocations and shocks, including the possibility of unemployment, inflation, and interregional and interindustry income differentials. The Soviet leadership wishes to shield workers from the worst of these consequences, but the costs of developing an extensive social welfare system may prove prohibitive.

Although the Soviet budget deficit is a major source of inflationary pressures, convertibility may impose additional pressures on state expenditures for social security and the temporary subsidization of industries facing competition from imports.

Thus, in addition to dealing with technical issues of international trade and finance, any proposal for ruble convertibility must deal with the domestic issues of creating markets, reforming prices, and bringing inflation under control, as well as set out a timetable to coordinate domestic and foreign trade reforms.

II. THE DOMESTIC ENVIRONMENT FOR RUBLE CONVERTIBILITY

A marketization of the Soviet Union's external economic relations by means of a convertible ruble is only possible if the domestic economy also functions along market principles. Thus, ruble convertibility will require, and also simultaneously assist, the implementation of far-reaching reforms of the Soviet economic system. As is well known, up to now these reforms have not been very successful and have not yielded the expected results; if this situation continues, achieving ruble convertibility in the near future is virtually impossible.

One may distinguish three main sets of problems that are currently the focus of the discussions of economic reforms in the Soviet Union and that simultaneously have direct implications for convertibility.

A. How Radical Are Economic Reforms?

Truly radical reforms in the Soviet economy are associated by many Soviet economists with a transition to a type of economic system that is known as market socialism. In such a system, state-owned firms, managed by their workers or by state-appointed managers, cooperatives, and private enterprises make the basic economic decisions about what to produce, where to sell their product, and what price to charge, while the government regulates the market primarily through fiscal, financial, and monetary policy means.

The transition to a market socialist economy means that the present system of directive planning has to be dismantled: *goszakazy* (government orders) must become voluntary instead of obligatory for enterprises. Rationed supply has to be replaced by wholesale trade, and prices have to be deregulated. This, in turn, implies that there must be a considerable redistribution of economic power, away from industrial departments and regional authorities and toward the enterprises. It also implies that huge collective and state farms in agriculture will be largely replaced by family farms, and that the conditions for the development of all types of cooperatively and individually owned enterprises must be created.

Progress toward such a reform has been hampered by two factors. The first is that both among Soviet economists and among the population at large there has been no consensus on the type of economic reform that is needed. Many would prefer to retain a major role for the government in setting the prices of industrial inputs and raw materials and issuing production forecasts and orders for individual goods. Such a system is incompatible with convertibility because it cannot provide for the free convertibility of rubles into goods, thus perpetuating commodity inconvertibility of the ru-

ble. The second factor slowing reform is the slowness with which
reforms are put into practice. Until recently, bureaucratic resistance has kept even those measures approved by the party leadership, the government, and the Supreme Soviet from being fully
implemented. If this bureaucratic resistance is not overcome in the
near future, then there is no hope that the reforms in the domestic
economy will yield the desired results.

To succeed, economic reform measures must be considered as an
integrated set of measures, and their implementation must be swift
and decisive, while taking into account the need to allow the economy to adjust to new forces and ways of functioning.

B. Monetary Issues

A marketizing reform in the Soviet Union will place a heavy burden on the country's currency because the ruble must replace the
plan as the principal means of transmitting economic information
and stimulating the activities of workers and producers. For this
task, the ruble has grown increasingly less useful, and sweeping
changes in policy will be required.

Currently, the overhang of undesired holdings of rubles on the
part of the population is growing rapidly. This is due in part to a
government budget deficit that has grown at an unprecedented rate
in the last decade. Official reporting projects the 1989 government
budget deficit in excess of 120 billion rubles, about 13.8 percent of
GNP.[1] The Soviet deficit is thus a significant source of inflationary
pressure in the Soviet economy. To make matters worse, the deficit
has been financed by printing money, so that the amount of money
in circulation continues to increase and now is three times greater
than the average level of the mid-1970s.

These inflationary pressures also fuel, and at the same time are
reinforced by, inflationary tendencies in the enterprise sector.
Paradoxically, reforms giving enterprises greater rights to set the
level of wages have contributed to these problems, largely because of
the failure to implement corresponding reforms in the sphere of

---

1. "Soviet Aide Discloses Debt, Says Budget Gap Worsens," *Wall Street Journal*,
August 7, 1989.

enterprise finance and especially to impose strict market discipline and the possibility of bankruptcy for unprofitable firms. As a result, the income of the population in 1988 exceeded plan targets by more than 20 billion rubles, due mainly to increases in salaries by more than 14.5 billion rubles. Such increases in income were not accompanied by equivalent increases in either labor productivity or the output of goods and services. Reported production increases mainly reflected official and unofficial price increases rather than advances in production. As a result of these wage increases and the printing of money to cover the government deficit, the amount of cash and savings deposits held by the population is five times greater than available stocks of consumer goods.

In an economy where most consumer goods prices are set by the government at an artificially low level, the gap between money demand and supply of goods manifests itself not only in price increases, but also in the increased shortages of goods. In fact, the inflation rate in the Soviet economy is still rather low, 3-5 percent as measured by the consumer price index. But if one considers the increase in the gap between money demand and the supply of goods and the increase in shortages, which is not reflected in the official price index, then the rate of depreciation of the ruble in terms of domestic purchasing power may be estimated to be at a level of 10-15 percent per year in recent years.

This latter rate of depreciation is actually the critical one, as it causes the conditions for the development of a cumulative inflationary process to emerge. Consumers try to get rid of unwanted money by buying tangible assets and goods, which leads to money velocity increases, feeds the devaluation process, and provides additional momentum for it. At this stage, even if the money printing machine is stopped and there is no increase in the money supply, inflation can be out of control.

In such a highly inflationary atmosphere, all economic incentives and instruments, such as taxes, subsidies, prices, and interest rates, become inefficient, and the whole idea of regulating economic activity through the use of these instruments becomes impossible. In this case, the government risks losing control over the economy, and strong pressures for the restoration of direct administrative methods of management may emerge as economic methods become inefficient. The clearest evidence of this is the fact that

Soviet authorities have postponed a reform of the price structure precisely because any conceivable reform must result in significantly
higher prices. Without market determined prices, neither reform nor convertibility are possible, but neither radical reform nor
full convertibility can be long-lasting or effective in an environment dominated by open inflation.

C. Creating a Socialist Market

The creation of a socialist market requires much more than simply
freeing prices and permitting enterprises to make decisions on
what, how, and for whom to produce. Both the ways in which the
enterprise sector and the economy as a whole will function must be
reconsidered.

A reform of the enterprise sphere must create new types of enterprises and alter the principles on which existing enterprises
function. Private and cooperative enterprise must be given greater
scope and security, both in industry and services and in agriculture.
Currently, attitudes toward such forms of production units are am-
bivalent; their legal status is uncertain, and a good deal of hostility
has been engendered by their high profits, their alleged orientation toward short-term and speculative activities, and their consequent unwillingness to invest these profits in expanding their activities. Many participants in this project felt that high profits
could be eliminated if a more secure legal status for private and cooperative enterprise could be created. This would increase the
number of private firms and the competition among them and create a greater willingness among co-operants and private entrepreneurs to invest. Moreover, a capital market must be established to channel profits of cooperatives and private entrepreneurs
who do not wish to expand their operations into other socially useful investments. Profit-making per se must come to be seen as a socially useful activity.

State enterprises also must function along new lines. Rather
than seeking to meet state orders or objectives, managers appointed
by the state must be given incentives to maximize the profitability
of their enterprises; those enterprises converted to labor-managed
firms will select their own manager, who will be encouraged by

the workers to maximize income per employee, an objective sufficiently close to profit maximization. A most important aspect of the reform will be to minimize the subsidies provided to state-owned enterprises and to make those subsidies that are provided as general as possible so as to avoid the subsidization of individual firms or groups of firms on the basis of special pleading.

Those public-sector firms that are unable to earn a profit must be forced to go bankrupt. Efforts should always be made to sell or lease failing firms either to their own workers or to cooperative or private investors, either domestic or foreign. The critical issue is to make managers responsible for profitable operation and to avoid the drain on government expenditures caused by the subsidization of inefficient enterprises.

A set of institutions must also be created to promote the efficient use of capital and to efficiently transfer it to sectors where it can earn the highest return. While a commercial banking sector is an important component of such a capital market, it is clearly insufficient, primarily because not all capital needs can be efficiently met by bank loans. Thus, provisions should be made to greatly expand and strengthen the rights of state, cooperative, and private enterprises to issue bonds and stocks. While some thought should be given to regulating such issues to avoid fraud and financial indiscipline, it would probably be wise to permit local securities markets and institutions to evolve on their own, rather than to attempt to legislate into existence some form of government-run stock and bond exchanges.

Finally, policies must be developed to promote competition on the domestic market, both among firms and interregionally. The emerging market economy in the Soviet Union will inevitably be highly monopolized. In a typical market for industrial products, there are currently just a few large enterprises that control the major part of total output; this is even more so in the case of transportation, communication, public utilities, and so on. That means that the market for these goods and services will be oligopolistic, and well-known oligopolistic effects will emerge. Producers may seek to reduce output while increasing prices, and the economy may face a sort of stagflation—falling output with high inflation.

This kind of a stagflation may well be occurring now, as the importance of state orders and production quotas for enterprises declines, and the enterprises get greater freedom to decide on their own what to produce. Managers of some industrial enterprises have revealed their desire to reduce output, increase their price, and thus increase the value of their output. The enterprises were going to do this even under the present conditions, when strict control over prices is exercised by the state pricing committee and industrial departments. It is reasonable, therefore, to expect that, as soon as the role of state orders is reduced considerably, there will be a real danger that the Soviet economy will enter a stagflation period, which will create an unfavorable domestic environment for any steps toward ruble convertibility.

To avoid such a development, it is necessary to put in effect a special set of policies designed to regulate the oligopolistic market. There is a need for antitrust legislation; for a vigorous competition policy aimed at dismantling the existing monopolies where possible; and for promoting the competitive structure of markets, in part by encouraging the entry of private and cooperative and labor-managed firms.

In the transition period to market socialism, it will be necessary to enact a system of tariffs on imports and a system of quotas on exports. These will be necessary to avoid excessive disruption of the domestic market as prices adjust from current state-controlled levels to those determined by markets. After this adjustment, the state may, of course, continue to maintain tariffs to influence the commodity structure of trade and the resulting pattern of domestic production.

The conception of a fiscal and monetary policy that would permit the government to influence the level of economic activity must be developed. While the general effects of changes in government spending and taxes and open market operations are generally well understood for capitalist market economies, this does not necessarily mean that such instruments would be as effective in a socialist market economy. The diminished effectiveness of macroeconomic policy may arise from differences in institutions, in the objectives of enterprises, or in disproportions among the economic size of the government, the state enterprise sector, and the private and cooperative sector. Moreover, the appropriate institutions, mechanisms, and trained personnel to pursue appropriate macroeconomic policies do not currently exist. Without these policies and people, the

transition to a market economy will be associated with the creation
of enormous disproportions that may eventually ruin the entire
economy, not to mention ruble convertibility.

Another area where new mechanisms and policies are badly
needed is social issues. The transition to a market economy will
inevitably be associated with the major redistribution of workers
among industries and regions; with temporary increases in
unemployment as many people change their jobs; and with accelerated and uneven price increases and growing income inequali-
ties. That means that the whole system of labor force training and
retraining, as well as the whole social security system, will experience great pressure. The truth is that, in their current state,
these systems and institutions are unequal to the demands that will
be placed on them. Reforms are needed to improve the employee
retraining system; to introduce unemployment insurance; to protect low-income groups by establishing an insurance and allowance
program and by the indexation of pensions; and to change the tax
system. In short, all these regulatory mechanisms must play a role
as a kind of safeguard that allows society to minimize the costs of a
market and to take full advantage of its benefits.

D. Policies for Radical Reform

The main barrier to the implementation of a radical reform in
the Soviet Union is the need to resolve the problems of the inflationary overhang of money in the hands of the public, and, at the
same time, to eliminate state orders and interference in interenterprise transactions and to reform the price-setting mechanism so
that markets, rather than bureaucrats, set prices. As described
above, part of the monetary overhang stems from the government's
deficit and part from the growth of wages in excess of increases in
the availability of consumer goods.

1. Equilibrating the Economy First . . .

One possible way of dealing with the overhang is to eliminate further inflationary money creation and to absorb excess savings by

increasing the supply of consumer goods. Once this is achieved, prices can be freed. Because there will be little remaining excess purchasing power, such a price reform will realign relative prices, with the price of some goods going up and the price of others going down, but there will be no tendency for the overall level of prices to increase sharply.

Some participants believed that this would be the best course of action. They pointed to the fact that the Soviet government plans to cut the budget deficit by 29 billion rubles in 1989 and by 34 billion rubles in the next year. At the same time, it is planned to increase production of consumer goods in 1990 in comparison with 1989 by more than 45-50 billion rubles. To achieve this target, the average rate of increase in the supply of consumer goods on a yearly basis would be five times greater than during the last three years. Cuts in government expenditure will be realized in defense and space programs as well as in subsidies, while revenues will be augmented by changes in tax laws and by a relaxation of the anti-alcohol campaign. The increase in the supply of consumer goods will be brought about in large part by lowering the volume of investment. But even if these ambitious objectives were reached, domestic markets would still be characterized by excess demand and shortages. Therefore, proponents of this option suggest further measures. Among these are:

a. financing the government deficit through the sale of bonds to the public. It is argued that such bond sales would be less inflationary than printing money to cover expenditures;
b. selling government-owned apartments, land, equipment, and other assets to the population; and
c. importing large amounts of western consumer goods for a period of years. The hard currency to purchase these goods would be obtained by borrowing in the West, possibly up to US$15-16 billion in the first year and US$5-6 billion a year subsequently.

If successful, these measures would allow a transition from a disequilibrated, "shortage" economy to one where aggregate demand and supply were in equilibrium and where the necessary price reform would not entail any inflation. Those participants who advocate the use of foreign borrowing to provide the funds needed to finance the transition to a market economy point to the fact that the internal debt at the moment is negligible, the value of government bonds held by the population is less than 10 billion rubles, and the external debt is not at all great. Net Soviet indebtedness in hard currency was approximately US$20 billion at the beginning of 1989, and, besides, the Soviet Union is in a position of net creditor toward a number of socialist and developing countries. These credits are mainly in rubles and in other inconvertible currencies, so they are not convertible into hard currency, but they still exist, and there may be a way to convert at least some of them into hard currency at some exchange rate as the ruble becomes convertible.

Those who advocate foreign borrowings also point to the fact that if economic reforms are truly radical, it will be possible to repay the debt, or at least to service it, as the efficiency of the economy increases. For example, a radical reform in agriculture, including voluntary dismantling of many collective and state farms and elimination of *goszakaz* and rationed supply, should bring about considerable increases in agricultural production, so that it will be possible to save hard currency, several billion dollars annually, which is currently being spent on food imports.

In short, foreign borrowings would allow the Soviet Union to minimize the costs of a transition period and to make the transition to an efficient market economy without major sacrifices in living standards. This is seen as a desirable and real option, under the condition that all the necessary measures are implemented simultaneously in a package: radical reforms, strict limits on monetary expansion, creation of regulatory mechanisms for a new type of market economy, and imports of consumer goods financed by external borrowings.

If such a reform can be brought about, then in five to seven years, at most, perestroika would pay for itself, as the efficiency of a new market economy would be considerably higher than that of the present system of direct planning. The current Soviet system is extremely wasteful in the sense that, due to enormous losses, a huge gap exists between production and consumption. The Soviet economy needs to produce roughly 1.5 times as much as does a market economy to provide the same level of consumption and living standards. In the United States, for example, net investment absorbs 6-

7 percent of national income, while the comparable figure is 25-30 percent in the Soviet Union. Allowing for the differences in the relative size of military expenditures in both countries, it turns out that the share of consumption in Soviet national income is hardly more than 50 percent, while in the United States it is more than 85 percent. If the Soviet economy can manage to take the transition to a market economy and thus reduce these losses to a level of an average market economy, it will be possible, using the same volume of inputs (that is, the same technology, the same labor force, the same amount of investments and resources), to increase living standards by approximately 1.5 times, entirely on the basis of better management and the improved ability to put resources together in a more efficient way. In this five- to seven-year transition period to a market economy, it would be possible to increase considerably the efficiency of the whole system, so that the economic restructuring would in fact produce higher levels of consumption in the long run without short-term sacrifices in living standards. The major problem, then, is to handle properly the economy during the transition period itself, obtaining the resources needed to finance the costs of transition; that is, to finance the government budget deficit without money emission and to increase expenditure for social purposes, such as the social security system and retraining of employees.

Although such a strategy to equilibrate the economy before proceeding to a price reform does offer a seemingly painless and thus politically appealing means of reforming the Soviet economy, a number of participants raised serious objections to the viability of the proposal. Among the objections raised were:

a. Estimates of the excess savings of the population are highly speculative. Therefore, we have no basis for judging whether proposed increases in the supply of consumer goods will actually eliminate, rather than merely ameliorate, shortages of goods.
b. Issuing government bonds to finance the government's deficit is not anti-inflationary. Advocates of this view argue from a faulty analogy with market economies where such "open market operations" do have anti-inflationary effect. However, the Soviet Union's banking system is entirely dif-

ferent, and thus the effect of bond sales on the money supply is not the same as in a market economy.

c. Reducing shortages through imports may reduce the pressure for radical reform, slowing the reform process. As a result, the Soviet economy may find itself with an economy only partially reformed but heavily in debt.

d. Buying decisions of firms and consumers alike will be based on the current, distorted price structure, leading to incorrect import decisions.

e. Reforms may take time to bear fruit, and thus the anticipated gains in productivity and output may be reaped only well after the foreign debt repayment begins. Thus, Soviet consumers may be better off in the short run as the result of imports, but they will suffer in the future when their consumption must fall to repay the debt.

f. Several participants pointed to the case of Poland, which also borrowed extensively in the West with the expectation that gains in productivity could provide the wherewithal to repay borrowing for imports of both capital and consumer goods.

2. . . . Or Eliminating Money Hoards?

Those participants who did not believe that the economy could be completely equilibrated by increasing domestic production and imports of consumer goods argued that some reforms of the monetary system should be employed instead of or alongside a policy of equilibration. Among the possibilities suggested were:

a. Freeing prices and letting a burst of inflation eliminate unwanted money stocks. In this way, the market would be created and would yield an appropriate price level and available set of relative prices. As long as the government and enterprises were constrained from further inflationary actions, the burst of inflation would be short-lived, and price stability could be established quickly.

There were a number of objections to this course of action. First, a high level of inflation was seen as being politically unacceptable, both because of general resistance to inflation among Soviet workers, and also because of equity implications for those living on fixed incomes. The inflationary process was also seen as being potentially cumulative and uncontrollable. Finally, some participants argued that resource allocations in an inflationary environment (for example, investments in unproductive assets such as collectibles and speculation) would be both harmful to the public's perception of the desirability and equity of the reform and economically unsound.

b. Reforming the currency by issuing a new ruble to replace the old one. In such a currency reform, each person could convert, say, 10 old rubles into 1 new ruble up to some amount. Beyond that amount, a less favorable exchange rate, for example 100 old rubles to 1 new ruble, would apply. In this way, excess cash hoards would be eliminated while protecting low- and fixed-income individuals from a loss of purchasing power. Freeing markets after such a reform would not result in excessive inflationary pressures.

Such a currency reform has been implemented in the past by a number of countries, including the Soviet Union. Nevertheless, several participants raised doubts about its political palatability and feasibility. Such a currency reform is viewed as unacceptable to the Soviet population and also as arbitrary in its effects on those who hold their wealth in cash and those who hold it in the form of real assets. The feasibility of the reform was also questioned, because foreknowledge of the imminent exchange of old rubles for new ones would lead to massive dishoarding and chaos on consumer markets.

c. Developing a new currency that would circulate alongside the ruble. The Soviet Union could create a new currency, for convenience called here a new ruble, that would circulate alongside the old ruble. The new currency would go into circulation gradually, through wage payments and government transfer payments to the population. The new ruble could be used to purchase certain categories of goods, including imported consumer goods, whose prices would be set by free markets. Other goods, possibly those whose prices would remain fixed at current levels, would be available for new rubles, as well as for old rubles at the same price. To the extent that holders of old rubles wished to reduce their hoards of this currency, they could trade them for new rubles and thus obtain goods not available for old rubles, though, of course, at considerably higher prices. As markets for various consumer goods move toward equilibrium, the distinction between old and new rubles would disappear. In the meantime, however, cash hoards will have been dissipated. The social cost would be the increase in the prices of goods available only for new rubles, but those individuals with low or fixed incomes could continue to obtain necessities at state-controlled prices through this transition period.

E. Conclusions

As in any complex economic question, there are disagreements over how best to proceed. Nevertheless, the participants of this proposal are in surprising harmony on the basic points. We believe that the prerequisites for full convertibility of the ruble that the domestic economy must meet include a radical and rapid marketizing reform; the creation of new forms of enterprises and of institutions to support the market mechanism and to take full advantage of its potential; and the establishment of a balance between demand and supply on internal markets in the most equitable and least disruptive way. It is only on the means of bringing this last condition about that we disagree. On this matter, then, we would suggest that further study is required to see whether some combination of existing proposals might be most appropriate or whether new means need to be sought out.

III. ACHIEVING RUBLE CONVERTIBILITY

If efforts to make the ruble convertible were to be delayed until the domestic economy was equilibrated and internal markets were functioning smoothly, then foreign trade would have made only a minor contribution to perestroika. The challenge is to consider ways in which some limited or partial forms of convertibility can be introduced before all the domestic prerequisites described in the foregoing section have been met. In this way, a closer interaction between some parts of the Soviet economy and the rest of the world can be established, furthering the progress of reforms within the Soviet Union and ensuring that progress toward convertibility keeps pace with domestic reform.

A. Current Developments in Soviet Foreign Trade Reforms

Before discussing what should be done to make the ruble convertible, it is necessary to first understand the foreign trade reforms that the Soviets are introducing now or contemplating for the near future. The main document at our disposal on the intentions of the Soviet government is the Decree of December 2, 1988, "On the Development of the Foreign Trade Activities of the State, Cooperative and Other Social Enterprises, Associations and Organizations." The main features of the decree seek to decentralize trade decisions and to move toward the convertibility of the ruble.

1.   The decree aims at expanding the foreign trade activities of the Soviet enterprises, at simplifying the rules for such activities, and at developing "monetary-market relations," which means the replacement of plans with price and profit signals (Introduction).
2.   It urges several institutions—Gosbank, Vnesheconombank, the Ministry of Finance—to prepare, during the first part of 1989, "concrete proposals for a step-by-step development of a partial convertibility of the Soviet ruble into foreign currencies" (Article 38).
3.   It announces a shift toward a realistic rate of exchange (Article 12):

> . . . to increase the participation of the U.S.S.R. in the international division of labor, to deepen the integration processes, in particular when new forms of cooperation are concerned, to make more meaningful the evaluation of export and import efficiency, a new rate of exchange will be introduced beginning from January 1, 1991, for settlements linked with foreign economic operations.

4. As a transitional measure (Article 13):

> . . . . before the shift toward accounting with a new rate of exchange, and beginning from January 1, 1990, there will be a 100% bonus to the rate of exchange of the free convertible currencies against the ruble.

A distinction is made between preparing the convertibility and introducing a new rate of exchange. The steps toward convertibility have yet to be officially defined, while the decision to introduce a new rate of exchange has been taken, although it remains for Gosbank, the Ministry of Finance, Gosplan, and the Vnesheconombank to decide upon the magnitude, the fixing procedure, and the uses of this new rate (Article 12, Paragraph 2). But clearly both processes are linked. The 100-percent bonus mentioned in Article 13 is to be applied to the conversion of the hard currency earnings of Soviet enterprises into rubles.

5. Some Soviet enterprises are to be able to retain a portion of their hard currency earnings from export operations. They may use such earnings to import western machinery and equipment, to import western consumer goods for their workers, or to sell their hard currency for rubles to other Soviet enterprises at officially organized currency auctions.

6. A new customs tariff will be implemented in 1991. Until the price reform is carried through, this new tariff, supplemented by more flexible import taxes and export quotas, will serve to bridge the gap between world and domestic prices. Tariffs will be highest (80-90 percent *ad valorem*) for consumer manufacturers and lowest for raw materials.

To understand the implications, let us assume that Soviet authorities follow the scenario more or less outlined in the 1988 decree:

First Step: In 1990, the ruble is "devalued" and there are no longer currency coefficients for calculating in domestic rubles the earnings in hard currencies of the Soviet enterprises. There is also a beginning of internal convertibility, through currency auctions. Through these auctions, we have a rate of exchange of the ruble against hard currencies (for the sake of brevity, let us assume that this is a rate of the ruble against the dollar) that strongly "devalues" the ruble in comparison with the new exchange coefficient. Let us call f_{off} the present official value of the dollar in rubles; f_{bon} ("bonified") the value of the dollar in rubles beginning from January 1, 1990; and f_{auc} the value of the dollar in rubles as it is bound to emerge from the auctions held in 1990, if not before.

We shall have: $f_{bon} = 2f_{off}$ (through the "bonus" of 100 percent). Should the present rate of exchange still be valid on December 31, 1989, we would get $f_{bon} = 2 (0.64)$, that is, 1 dollar would earn 1.28 rubles to the enterprise exporting in dollars.

But of course we must be aware of the fact that the enterprise was not getting f_{off} for 1 dollar exported in 1989. It was getting f_{off} modified by a "DCC" (differentiated currency coefficient), according to the goods exported and presumably also according to their destinations. The DCCs now range from 0.2 to 6.6. Thus, because the enterprise receives for each dollar of exports rubles worth its DCC x f_{off}, some enterprises receive as little as 0.128 rubles (0.64 x 0.2) for each dollar of exports, while others receive 4.224 rubles (0.64 x 6.6) for each dollar of their exports. It is widely believed that for most transactions the average value of the DCC is more than 2. If we call $f_{mod} = $ DCC f_{off}, then if DCC > 2, $f_{mod} > f_{bon}$; that is, the January 1, 1990, measure will amount to a revaluation, and not a devaluation. In this case, enterprises will not be encouraged to export to the West. It will be necessary to devise some additional measures, such as subsidies, to create the appropriate incentives.

One such incentive for exporting manufactured goods, which currently benefit from relatively high DCCs, will be the ability of exporting enterprises to retain some part of their hard currency earnings. Such retained export earnings can be used to import equipment or consumer goods from the West. The consumer goods can be sold to the enterprises' workers at prices that imply a more favorable exchange rate than f_{bon}, thus boosting the enterprise's effective ruble/dollar exchange rate. Alternatively, the enterprise can choose to sell its hard currency to another enterprise through a currency auction, again at a rate exceeding f_{bon}.

In their first phase, the hard currency auctions will be open to selected Soviet enterprises and only much later expanded to a broader range of state enterprises, to joint ventures, and eventually to cooperative and private enterprises. The ruble/dollar rate of exchange emerging from auctions will naturally be tantamount to a very large "devaluation" of the ruble. Thus, according to our terminology, $f_{auc} > f_{bon}$. By how much? Should the present rate of exchange on the black market constitute an upper limit, we would have $f_{auc} = 11.7\ f_{bon}$, since the black market rate of exchange is up to 15 rubles for 1 dollar.

The incentives provided by the possibility of importing western goods or auctioning off hard currency earnings will be offset to some extent by the introduction of new, higher tariffs on imports that will bear most heavily on consumer goods. Until domestic prices in the Soviet Union are reformed, additional import taxes will have to be employed to prevent too great a difference between domestic and world prices and to reflect the fact that at the bonus rate the ruble will continue to be very overvalued relative to western currencies.

A number of features of this interim system were viewed favorably by most participants:

1. The elimination of differentiated currency coefficients was considered to be a useful precursor to a system where domestic and foreign prices could be compared and thus serve as a basis for both domestic price reforms and for import and export decisions.
2. Hard currency retention and auctions represent a very limited form of internal convertibility because some holders of rubles are now able to convert them into hard currency and to exercise some freedom of choice in their hard currency expenditures.
3. The auctions provide information about the international value of the ruble.
4. The auction process will help educate officials and managers about foreign exchange operations.

On the other hand, several participants believed that, as actually implemented, the positive potential of the interim measures has been largely wasted:

1. The volume of hard currency retained by firms is too small, and many of the Soviet Union's principal hard currency exports are not to be included in the scheme.
2. The auctions are extremely limited in scope, to the extent that it may not be valid to call them auctions at all. The number of bidders is to be limited, and their participation in the "auction" will be based on the foreign trade authorities' evaluation of the use that the bidders intend to make of the hard currency. Successful bids will be determined not by the price the bidder is willing to pay for hard currency, but rather on the basis of the economic results to be obtained from the machinery and equipment to be imported with the hard currency.
3. There is an odd dichotomy between the degree of convertibility enjoyed by firms earning hard currency through exports and those buying it at auction. The former are free to convert their money either into western consumer goods or into western machinery; the latter, only into western machinery and then only into machinery specified in their auction bid.

Thus, the market is too thin and too circumscribed to either provide much information about the ruble/dollar exchange rate or to give Soviet ruble holders any genuine convertibility into hard currencies.

Second Step: The decree is much more ambiguous about the next stage of the foreign trade reform, which involves the fixing of a realistic exchange rate of the ruble. Nothing is specified about currencies in which this exchange rate is to be denominated and about the use of this exchange rate. Nevertheless, four hypotheses are sufficiently plausible to warrant discussion:

Hypothesis 1. The fixing of an exchange rate is a step toward the convertibility of the ruble. In this case, and looking at the provisions of Article 12 of the decree, we may expect the envisioned convertibility to have the following features:

1. It will presumably be a "commercial" rather than a "financial" convertibility, and also a "current account" rather

than a "capital account" (see the wording "a rate for settlements linked with foreign economic operation").

2. Assuming that the new rate is fixed against all currencies in which the Soviet Union has foreign economic settlements, the convertibility of the ruble might be achieved vis-à-vis the socialist currencies, as well as vis-à-vis the transferable ruble. But unlike a convertibility in western currencies, the relevant decisions cannot be taken by the Soviet Union alone. The Soviet Union has to reach an agreement with part or all of its CMEA partners. Therefore, the introduction of such a convertibility is a long way off for political rather than strictly economic reasons, while the obstacles to convertibility in hard currencies are mainly economic.

Hypothesis 2. The magnitude of the new rate of exchange will be such that it will amount to a devaluation of the ruble, even by comparison to the "devalued" rate introduced against hard currencies in 1990. The devaluation will be greater against hard currencies than against soft currencies. The need for such a devaluation stems from the fact that the "bonus" of 100 percent over the present official rate of exchange is too small to make a significant share of Soviet exports profitable at the present level of Soviet prices. According to several Soviet sources, it should be raised to a level where more or less 80 percent of Soviet exports would be profitable. This proportion is said to be acceptable and in line with what is done in other socialist countries. This, in turn, suggests that the Soviet authorities may wish to follow the practice of countries like Hungary or Poland, where the initial "commercial," as opposed to the meaningless official, rate of exchange was fixed at a sort of purchasing power parity rate calculated on a basket of representative export goods. The rate was said to express how much domestic money was needed to get a unit of foreign currency. Such a stance would not, however, be consistent with the aim of having an overall foreign exchange policy.

Hypothesis 3. The new rate of exchange of the ruble (f_{com} 1991) would be likely to remain administered by the foreign trade authorities once initially fixed. This means that neither currency auctions nor any form of currency market is going to determine further changes in the exchange rate (except as a broad indicator).

The most likely method to be applied would be, for convertible currencies, the "basket" method already used by the Gosbank; presently the official rate of exchange, f_{off}, is modified according to the fluctuations of a basket of the main currencies used in Soviet settlements. The decision to "devaluate" or "revaluate" the ruble further would be taken by the authorities upon given economic considerations. In any case, the price reform, when implemented, would bring about changes in the rate of exchange. It is not yet clear whether the rate of exchange will influence the price reform, that is, whether Soviet domestic prices are to be related to world prices.

Hypothesis 4. There are going to be multiple exchange rates by fields of application. For instance, f_{com} 1991 might be different for converting into rubles trade settlements in dollars with western partners, and settlements denominated in dollars within clearing agreements. There might also be a different rate for noncommercial operations, for tourists, for operations with joint ventures, and within special economic zones.

While it is impossible to judge which of the above, if any, hypotheses best describes what course Soviet authorities may follow, a number of participants argued that, aside from Hypothesis 1, none of these scenarios addresses the question of convertibility directly, and they all seem to be strangely disconnected from the interim measures. The following points were raised:

1. Hypothesis 1 provides for convertibility, but the economic obstacles for such a sweeping move make such convertibility impossible to achieve in the near future. Consequently, it cannot be viewed as a viable near-term measure unless domestic stabilization and reform proceed at a pace much faster than currently envisioned.

2. The other three hypotheses call for a more rational exchange rate, which would be very useful in linking domestic and foreign prices, but they do not imply that the ruble would be any more convertible, either for foreigners or for Soviet residents, than it is now. For example, Hungary has had a commercial exchange rate that better reflects the international purchasing power of the forint than did the official rate. While this may have helped Hungarian authorities to make better judgments

about Hungary's competitiveness in world markets, it has not led to forint convertibility.

3. None of these hypotheses makes an effective link to the measures introduced in the interim phase. The role of auctions and hard currency retention remains peripheral despite its potential for creating at least limited convertibility.

In light of these points, it can be argued that solutions already attempted in other socialist countries could help bring some greater rationality into Soviet trade decisions much as convertibility would. Nevertheless, achieving such an increase in trade efficiency is not the same thing as achieving convertibility; indeed, it is, in a way, a substitute for convertibility.

B. Moving Toward Ruble Convertibility

While not unanimous, a consensus emerged among the authors that greater progress toward ruble convertibility could be made by expanding the scope of hard currency auctions, so that they increasingly encompassed a greater volume of Soviet hard currency trade and permitted participation of a greater number and type of buyers and sellers. Eventually, the practice of holding periodic auctions would give way, in a quite natural and evolutionary manner, to a genuine foreign exchange market.

Phase 1. We believe that the first step toward achieving ruble convertibility in this way is to turn the currently bureaucratically rigged auctions into genuine auctions where the hard currency will go to the highest bidder. This means that a larger number of enterprises must be permitted to participate and that they must have greater freedom to determine how to utilize the hard currency they purchase. At this stage, tariffs, taxes, and quotas on exports may be needed to avoid dysfunctional behavior because prices will not have been reformed. Such a step has several advantages:

1. It would expand the convertibility of the ruble by giving ruble holders greater ability to purchase hard currencies and ultimately western goods.

2. More buyers might raise the price of hard currencies, but this
    would automatically stimulate Soviet enterprises to expand their
    exports to the West, creating a strong basis for a policy of
    "export-oriented" growth in the Soviet Union.
3. Managers would assume greater responsibility and thus no
    doubt moderate their demand for western equipment and in-
    puts as their real price, both in rubles and in foregone imports
    of western consumer goods for their workers, becomes more ev-
    ident.   Soviet lending authorities would have to exercise
    greater control over enterprise credit to prevent enterprises
    from borrowing rubles recklessly to purchase hard currencies.
    Such restraint would be beneficial, as it would serve to reduce
    financial indiscipline and force the authorities to make the
    possibility of bankruptcy real.

Phase 2. The auctions could eventually be broadened to include a
wider range of enterprises, particularly as prices in the Soviet
Union began to respond to market forces. Thus, not only firms exporting manufactured goods, but also firms exporting fuels, miner-
als, and natural resources, could be permitted to participate on this
market. Such participation would be contingent on a rationalization of Soviet prices that yielded more appropriate domestic prices
for these goods or on a continuation of tariffs and quotas for some
goods. Alternatively, the government could continue to export
these goods with distorted prices under the old system but auction
off the hard currency earned in these transactions. The government also ought to participate on the auction market as a buyer of
hard currency to meets its own needs for hard currency. In this
way, the government would expand the size of the market while
simultaneously becoming a major market participant with the
ability to stabilize the market through sales and purchases.

Phase 3. Once much of the hard currency receipts and requirements of the state sector are cleared through the auction system, cooperatives and private enterprises should also be permitted to participate. Because these business units are much smaller than state
enterprises, the character of the foreign exchange market must
change because it is unlikely that an auction mechanism will be
most appropriate. Rather, a genuine foreign exchange market
with daily fixings will develop. Large state enterprises may con-

tinue to participate in this market on their own account, but banks will increasingly play a role, buying and selling foreign exchange for the smaller cooperative and private enterprise clients. At this point, if not earlier, joint Soviet-western ventures may also be permitted to participate in the market.

Phase 4. In this phase, households may be given the right to hold foreign currencies. As with cooperative and private firms, households will not deal directly with the foreign exchange market, relying instead on the intermediation of financial institutions. In this way, the state can, if it wishes, operate a dual exchange rate, one for enterprises and another for households.

Once Phase 4 is completed, ruble convertibility for Soviet residents will have been achieved. Therefore, foreign and domestic prices will have been linked in a slow and controlled way that enables the authorities to cope with the unforeseen effects of liberalization in trade and in the domestic economy.

Phase 5. Finally, external convertibility, the ability of foreigners to hold and freely exchange rubles, can be achieved by permitting them access to the foreign exchange market. No doubt such external convertibility will apply mainly to current account transactions, because the ability of foreigners to purchase capital assets in the Soviet Union will remain circumscribed. Similarly, internal convertibility will be limited to the current account, as it is unlikely that Soviet enterprises and residents will be given the right to freely invest abroad.

Phase 1 of this proposal could be implemented within the space of one or two years, and a transition period to Phase 2 could follow for a period of four to five years. The transition to Phase 2 would depend very much on the pace of price reforms and on the ability to create free markets and to reduce bureaucratic interference with economic processes. Phase 3 ought not to be attempted before inflationary pressures within the domestic economy have been largely eliminated. Otherwise, cooperative and private businesses will become a conduit for converting unwanted rubles into hard currencies.

If Soviet timetables for internal reform are taken at face value, it would be possible to contemplate reaching Phase 3 by the year 2000 and Phase 4 before 2005. However, these time schedules are overly

optimistic to a number of participants, and they believe that the
process could take as much as twice as long as sketched.

Finally, as with proposals for domestic reform, participants
wished to stress certain implications of the proposal or to differ
with certain aspects of it. To some participants, the ability to
achieve a limited but real convertibility of the ruble in phases 1
and 2 is an effective counter to those in the Soviet Union who argue
that price reform must precede convertibility. In our proposal, convertibility is achieved—and at a low cost in economic rationality—
if an effective system of tariffs and import taxes and quotas is implemented to protect domestic producers in the transition period to a
market economy. Thus, the differences between Soviet and foreign
prices should not serve as a pretext for delaying these first steps toward convertibility.

Some participants also believed that external convertibility could
be achieved as early as Phase 1, and that measures to bring about
the ability of foreigners to hold rubles and convert them to hard
currencies at this early stage were desirable. Advocates of this position feared that an early movement to convertibility for Soviet residents would undermine the ruble by diverting pent-up buying
power to the foreign exchange market. On the other hand, foreigners could be allowed to participate in very limited Phase 1
hard currency auctions. Even though few would be likely to avail
themselves of the opportunity of acquiring rubles unless the Soviet
government were to offer high interest bearing ruble assets, *de jure*
external convertibility would be achieved. Opponents of this view
argued that such purely financial convertibility would be of no practical use because foreigners would most likely seek to continue to
invoice their transactions with the Soviet Union in hard currencies, and because they would have little interest in holding rubles
whose value was determined on very limited and infrequent auctions.

IV. RUBLE CONVERTIBILITY: THE ROLE OF THE WEST

In this section, we examine what roles the United States, and to a
lesser extent other developed market economies, can play in the attempts to reform the Soviet economy, to integrate it more closely

into the world system of trade and payments, and to make its currency convertible.

A. The Role of the U.S. Government

The prospective role of the U.S. government in furthering reform in the Soviet Union that we propose here is based on several assumptions that need to be made explicit. The first of these is that the need to make fundamental changes in the Soviet economic system, changes that provide greater scope for market forces, increase reliance on the profit motive, give greater scope to private initiative, and expand the volume and nature of economic contacts with the West, is rooted in objective facts and is not the whim of one or several Soviet leaders. While the path to the realization that central planning is an increasingly dysfunctional economic system was perhaps slower and more tortuous in the Soviet Union than in some other planned economies, the evidence of its defects is overwhelming even if disagreement continues over viable alternatives. Thus, any Soviet leader must address the country's economic malaise, and some movement toward decentralization appears to be an inevitable component of such a reform.

The second assumption is that, if it is to be effective, economic reform must be accomplished by political reform. This is due in part to the fact that if economic rationality is to be real, it must be protected from being overridden by political expediency. Moreover, meaningful economic reform in the Soviet Union will of necessity be a process that will deeply stress the social fabric. Reform will entail inflation, unemployment, and changes in the distribution of incomes and of political and economic power with which the current political system will be unable to cope. Thus, social peace can be maintained only by combining the positive fruits of reform with a political liberalization that gives people the power to shape the reform process and apportion its costs and benefits.

A third assumption is that the process of reform will be a long one, marked by both progress and retreat. The realization that the reform process will be slow and difficult is critical because neither policymakers nor voters in the United States should mislead themselves into expecting excessively rapid change only to lapse into apathy or disappointment when such change is either not forthcoming or sometimes reversed. Government policies must be formulated for the long run and shaped to the needs of an incremental, if ultimately radical, reform.

Stemming from these assumptions is the final characteristic of Soviet-American relations in the future. Given the fragile nature of reform, its incremental pace of implementation, and the uncertainty that attends Gorbachev's ability to remain in power or of the Soviet political system to replace him in an open and orderly fashion, it is likely that the U.S. will wish to hedge its bets in supporting Soviet reform. Despite the cuts in troops and weapons already agreed to and under negotiation and the inward turn in Soviet foreign policy, the old zero-sum relationship of mistrust and power-balancing between the two nations is likely to color the thinking of political elites and voters alike. Thus, there will be strong incentives for the U.S. to seek measures that promote reform but that can be reversed easily and that do not leave U.S. interests and assets hostage to political and economic changes in the Soviet Union.

Within the limitations imposed by these assumptions, there are nevertheless useful policy options open to U.S. policymakers in the area of trade policy and in a number of other areas.

1. Import Policies

The primary policy barrier to Soviet exports to the United States is the Jackson-Vanik Amendment, which links the granting of a revocable form of most-favored nation (MFN) status to the Soviet Union and other East European countries to their emigration policies. The lack of MFN status is not a serious practical barrier to Soviet exports because these consist largely of raw materials, which are subject to low duties. It does, however, play an important psychological role in Soviet-U.S. trade and does limit the possibility for more creative forms of ventures between American businesses and Soviet enterprises. Moreover, because it is hard currency generated through sales of manufactures that is to be the basis of the first hard currency auctions in the Soviet Union, access to western markets for these goods is of great importance. The amendment has never been effective in positively influencing emigration in any of the target countries save Romania, and there only temporarily. Thus, repealing Jackson-Vanik would be appropriate given the political liberalization in the Soviet Union, while also providing a valuable psychological boost to trade between the two countries and opening the door to manufactures produced by western joint ventures in the Soviet Union.

Another barrier to Soviet exports to the United States is the uncertainty faced by centrally planned economies in dumping actions brought before the U.S. International Trade Commission (ITC). This uncertainty stems from the ITC's inability to compute either the cost or the domestic price of exports from centrally planned economies and the consequent need to adopt relatively arbitrary estimates of such data. In the short run, Soviet reforms are not likely to be extensive enough to obviate the problem, but it is to be hoped that the ITC will be cognizant of, and responsive to, the gradual convertibility of the ruble and the consequent linking of Soviet domestic and export prices. Quite clearly, the Soviet Union will have a role to play in promoting such responsiveness on the ITC's part; in the first instance by being sensitive to the dumping issue in its export decisions, and subsequently as it moves toward ruble convertibility by making the process as open and transparent to outsiders as possible.

The immediate impact of MFN status on the ability of the Soviet Union to export to the U.S. will be small. Nevertheless, its psychological impact would be important, not only by placing the Soviet Union on an equal footing with our other trading partners, but also by serving as a confidence-building measure for Soviet enterprises considering exporting to the United States and to U.S. businesses considering trade or joint ventures with Soviet partners. As the ruble becomes convertible at a more realistic value, the possibility of imports of manufactures from the Soviet Union will increase, and sensitivity on the part of both Soviet exporters and the ITC to potential conflicts and misunderstandings will be required.

2. Export Policies

In the past, the United States has used its control over exports to the Soviet Union and to other communist countries both as a carrot and a stick, either by reducing the severity of export restrictions or by curtailing access to U.S. goods. At times, such policies have succeeded, but all too often they have proven to be ineffective and even counterproductive.

The most sensitive issue has been the control of technology exports. Within the United States, controversy has raged around the length of time required to gain approval for such exports, the politicized and capricious nature of licensing decisions, and the adversarial relationship between the departments of Defense and Commerce in determining which goods should be exported. Internationally, the United States and its partners in COCOM have often disagreed on the appropriate extent of controls over technology exports to the Soviet Union and on the adequacy of the means for preventing the export of prohibited goods.

Some amelioration and rationalization of U.S. policy toward technology exports would assist in reform in the Soviet Union by facilitating the export of civilian-use technology by American firms. Nevertheless, the issue is a thorny one, and advocates of less restrictive policies will find it difficult to make headway on this issue. Nor can they expect much assistance from the Soviet Union; cases of Soviet industrial espionage and violations of export controls, such as the Toshiba case, will inevitably color policymakers' perceptions of Soviet objectives in importing western technology.

The United States has also attempted to use grain exports to influence or punish Soviet behavior. If the Soviet Union is to be encouraged to integrate itself into the international economy, then it ought to be able to perceive itself as not being forced to face such capricious external shocks. In the most recent grain agreement, the United States has agreed to refrain from such disruptions; whether this is due to greater political maturity or to the political influence of American farmers is unclear. Nevertheless, further assurances of the security of U.S. sources of supply would encourage the integration of the Soviet Union into the world economy.

3. Credit Policies

The United States restricts lending to the Soviet Union in two ways. First, Export-Import Bank (Ex-Im) credits to the Soviet

Union are limited by the so-called Stevenson Amendment. Because the Soviet Union is viewed by Ex-Im as a developed country, it is not eligible for subsidized credits. As a result, Ex-Im Bank lending is not competitive with alternative sources of trade finance that are currently available to the Soviet Union, and, therefore, the Stevenson Amendment is not a barrier to low-cost credit. The Ex-Im Bank also issues guarantees that protect lenders against business and political risks. Such guarantees may become useful if the volume of Soviet-American trade and investment increases. Consequently, the possibility of repealing the Stevenson Amendment should be considered, especially in the context of a general review of Soviet-American trade relations considered below.

Lending to the Soviet Union is also restricted by the Johnson Debt Default Act, which prohibits lending to countries that are in default of their loans to the United States unless such countries belong to the IMF or unless the Ex-Im Bank participates in the loan. The issue had been resolved by the 1972 U.S.-Soviet trade agreement, but, because the agreement was never implemented, further action must be taken if innovative forms of funding U.S. businesses operating in the Soviet Union are to be developed.

4. Joint Ventures

There are no specific government barriers to joint ventures between United States firms and Soviet enterprises, although, of course, there are restrictions on the flows of capital and technology to the Soviet Union and on the products of the joint ventures that would be re-exported to the United States. Nevertheless, as the volume of U.S. investment in the Soviet Union increases, there could well evolve a desire to formulate government policies to regulate such investment. A positive step would be to consider some form of insurance for American investors that would protect their investments in the Soviet Union against political and exchange risk. Political risk would largely take the form of expropriation or abrogation of stipulated rights of joint ventures to do business and to repatriate profits. Such risks could clearly arise if the reform movement were to be reversed or if joint ventures come to be less favorably viewed by the Soviet leadership. American investors in

joint ventures also face considerable exchange risk, partly because
the exchange rate is set by the Soviet government, and also because
both domestic excess demand and the hunger for foreign goods
within the Soviet Union suggest that the ruble is seriously overvalued and that any move to let it seek an equilibrium value could result in devaluation.

One possible way of dealing with this problem would be to
establish a binational or possibly a multinational insurance
scheme that would protect western joint-venture participants
against expropriation or the loss of business and repatriation rights
in the Soviet Union, against government-mandated devaluations of
the ruble, and perhaps against some market-generated exchange
risk. To make such an insurance scheme viable, the Soviet Union
would have to be a major participant, and it would have to contribute assets that were deposited in the West to make their
commitment credible. Despite this cost, the insurance program
would be an important confidence-building measure for western
investors and governments alike, and it would, in a limited sense,
establish the convertibility of the ruble for foreign joint-venture
participants.

5. Business Diplomacy

A final area for government policy would be to work in favor of developments in the Soviet Union that are favorable toward reform
and ruble convertibility. Such efforts should not be directed toward
influencing political developments in the Soviet Union. Efforts directed toward policymakers should rather focus on presenting, in a
clear and unbiased way, the views of American businesses on Soviet
economic policies. While such policies are ultimately the responsibility of Soviet officials, they are often formulated without a clear
understanding of the effect, positive or negative, on the ability of
western businesses to trade with or to invest in the Soviet Union.
Such representations are quite common among market economies,
but so far have been insignificant in our relations with the Soviet
Union.

The U.S. government should also consider policies at the grass-
roots level, providing assistance to emerging cooperatives and pri-

vate enterprises in industry, agriculture, and trade. More than material assistance, which would by necessity be minor, such firms will need basic information on business skills and technical matters and on their international market prospects. Thus, either formalized training programs or some form of CORE (Corps of Retired Executives) should be considered as legitimate forms of government activity. Similar programs could be developed for agriculture.

6. Actions to Take

The above policy issues are unlikely to be resolved independently of each other, largely because some, such as Jackson-Vanik, have political and emotional overtones that make it difficult to trade off economic and noneconomic issues. However, most of the policy barriers to improved prospects for Soviet-American trade could be negotiated as a single package that would resolve Soviet debts to the United States, the issue of MFN treatment for Soviet goods, the establishment of an insurance fund for joint ventures in the Soviet Union, and mechanisms for U.S. aid to private enterprises in the Soviet Union. Issues of access to the Soviet market for U.S. goods and investors, the convertibility of the ruble, and the opening of the Soviet economy should also be raised in such a negotiation. Within the context of such an overall normalization of commercial relations between the two countries, more could be achieved than in a piecemeal approach.

7. Areas of Difficulty

In considering a normalization of commercial relations between the Soviet Union and the United States, it must be recognized that political relations between the two countries now and in the foreseeable future carry much higher stakes for both sides than do economic considerations. Therefore, economic considerations will remain subordinate to political relations, and thus there are a number of areas of mutual interest that will have to be closely monitored.

East Europe. Although the Soviet Union appears to be disengaging itself from East Europe in economic terms, the extent and pace of this disengagement in political terms is as yet uncertain not only to the East Europeans but also to Soviet leaders themselves. The European Community is likely to serve as a strong magnet for East Europe, particularly as the Soviet Union also redirects its trade toward the West. Given the possibility of economic dislocation and political instability in these countries, it would be wise for the Soviet Union, the EC, and the United States to think more creatively about ways to stabilize both the economies and the political processes in these countries.

West Europe. For quite understandable reasons, the West European stake in trade with the Soviet Union and with East Europe is greater than that of the United States. While this has some positive features, there is also a danger, which stems largely from the tendency of the West European countries to view large export credits as a suitable answer to Soviet desires for economic integration into the world economy and to compete with each other for Soviet markets largely on the basis of their credit policies. Such an approach would be counterproductive. Massive borrowing by the Soviet Union would not resolve economic problems in that country; rather, it would in the long run exacerbate them, leading to a low-profit, opportunistic approach to East-West commerce, an approach that would not provide a stable basis either for ruble convertibility or for integration of the Soviet Union into the world economy.

Soviet Domestic Policy. The willingness of the United States to liberalize its trade with the Soviet Union will depend in large part on American perceptions of developments in the Soviet Union. As long as these are viewed as democratizing and marketizing, the U.S. attitude will be favorable. But, reform may spark unrest to the extent that force may be used against the population. The sharpness of western reaction to recent events in China suggests that strikes and ethnic unrest and the way in which the Soviet government deals with them have important foreign policy implications.

U.S. Domestic Policy. There is, of course, a school of thought in the United States that sees the Soviet Union's changed posture on economic reform, on national security, and on international relations as a tactic, one that will be abandoned when circumstances permit. Should such an approach gain ground, little progress in Soviet-American relations can be made.

Third World. Although Soviet-American tensions over many conflicts in developing countries have been de-escalating in recent years, many continue to fester. The American public and policy-makers tend to view Soviet behavior in such areas as a litmus test of Soviet intentions.

B. The Role of U.S. Business

Given the extent of the Soviet Union's economic problems and the size of its economy, the bulk of the resources for restoring internal and external equilibrium and thus creating the basis for convertibility of the ruble and the monetization of the economy must be generated internally. Nevertheless, there are important ways in which American businesses can contribute to bringing about ruble convertibility.

1. Creating a Business Climate in the Soviet Union

In the past, western business leaders have taken a passive policy toward Soviet trade policies and practices, accepting them as given and being content to work within them. In many cases, these practices and policies are ill-considered and severely restrict the volume of business between the two countries. Soviet joint-venture laws, for example, are vague, cumbersome, and stifle many potentially beneficial opportunities. It would be useful for the American business community to establish ways of developing suggestions for improvements in Soviet trade legislation and practices and bringing such suggestions to the attention of Soviet authorities.

American business could also do much to aid private, cooperative, and other market-oriented activities in the Soviet Union by actively seeking out collectives with which to do business and by providing training, internships, and educational materials to private-sector workers and managers. Similar technological and business aid could be provided to nonsocialized agricultural units.

2. Joint Ventures

While joint-venture opportunities should be considered on the basis of their profit potential, it must be recognized that such ventures represent a powerful means of spreading a market- and profit-oriented business culture within the Soviet economy, both among managers and workers. Thus, in formulating such ventures, U.S. firms must seek the greatest scope for market forces in the guidance of business operations and the greatest flexibility in rewarding workers and managers for their efforts. In this way, the knowledge and attitudes necessary for ruble convertibility can be established more rapidly.

C. International Organizations

At this time, and in the next decade, there is not a great role for international organizations to play in bringing about ruble convertibility or integrating the Soviet Union into the world economy. This is due in part to the fact that the current nonintegration of the Soviet and world economies is largely the result of Soviet policies and of their economic system. To change these is largely an internal matter. Also, current Soviet participation in international organizations is a matter of calculating the costs and benefits of such membership. In many cases, the benefits are minor, while the costs of trying to live up to the requirements and rules of these international organizations may stifle the reform of the economy and limit the reformers' ability to act creatively.

1. The GATT

Although the Soviet Union has approached the GATT, there seems to be little enthusiasm among GATT members for considering Soviet membership. Clearly, experiences with Poland and Romania have shown that formulas based on quantities are unsatisfactory, and the Soviet trade mechanism at this point is not consistent with any other means of granting benefits to GATT members.

2. The IMF

The Soviet Union is less interested in the IMF, though it and the
World Bank have expertise that would be valuable in establishing
a convertible currency and the institutions needed to sustain it.
The Soviet Union should consider ways of associating itself with
these institutions that would not necessarily require full membership but that would enable the Soviet Union to contribute to the
work of these organizations and at the same time tap their considerable expertise in trade and financial reform.

CHAPTER 6

Ruble Convertibility in the Reform Process: A Sobering Note

JOZEF M. VAN BRABANT

INTRODUCTION

With the possible exception of consideration of the virtues or draw-backs of central planning in a centrally planned economy (CPE), few economic topics have been written about more or understood less than convertibility. Although the issue flared up occasionally in the decades preceding the current wholesale wave of East European reforms, since the start of perestroika in the Soviet Union there has been a quantum leap in pamphleteering about currency convertibility and the use of a convertible transferable ruble as the key to promoting socialist economic integration in the near future.

Although I am very skeptical about the economic rationale most observers claim is at the foundation of this leap forward in think-ing about convertibility, I do not intend to repeat what I previously said on the subject. This paper uses the recent debate in CPEs on national and regional currency convertibility as a backdrop for some sobering normative reminders about the requirements and prevailing opportunities for convertibility.

Section I, as unambiguously as possible, illuminates the concept of convertibility and the ongoing debate. Section II discusses the benefits and costs of convertibility. Section III briefly summarizes

The views expressed here are my own and do not imply expression of any opinion whatsoever on the part of the United Nations Secretariat.

the schools of thought on convertibility. Section IV sketches the starting position for reforms in the CPEs, placing the principal emphasis on the trade and payments regimes of these countries. Section V summarizes the national and regional measures and their bearing on the evolving trade and payments regimes. Section VI evaluates the gap between what presently prevails or might soon come about and the fundamental requirements for using convertibility as a means of ensuring market-oriented resource allocation. The preconditions for realizing the advantages of convertibility while minimizing its drawbacks are also discussed. Finally, the paper concludes with a sketch of a variant of the European Payments Union that may be explored as a model for laying the foundations for convertibility, first perhaps within the Council for Mutual Economic Assistance (CMEA) and later in the East-West context.

I. ON THE CONCEPT OF CONVERTIBILITY

Simply put, convertibility is the ability of some classes of holders of one currency to exchange it against another or to transform it into goods on demand. I use "some classes" to remain realistic while not imposing restrictions on the ability of some classes to convert their money holdings. Let me explain these qualifiers.

Since World War II, convertibility for most countries essentially has corresponded to the definition in Article VIII of the Articles of Agreement of the International Monetary Fund. Contrary to what sometimes is quoted in the literature, Section 2 of that article states explicitly that "no member shall, without the approval of the Fund, impose restrictions on the making of payments and transfers for current international transactions" (IMF 1978, 29).

In practice, however, Article VIII convertibility has been understood to apply mainly to current account transactions by nonresidents in consequence of the regulation of relations between member banks of the Fund in Section 4 of Article VIII (IMF 1978, 30). Restrictions on current account transactions of residents are condoned provided the banking system does not unduly inhibit commercial payments (Edwards 1985, 390-91). However, precisely what a current transaction is and what it is not is not clearly spelled out in the legal sense.   By a recent count, 61 members of the International Monetary Fund fall under Article VIII's regime, but that does not mean, of course, that all adhere to the formal obligations; in fact, some may be using a *de facto* multiple exchange rate system (IMF 1988).

Many countries also apply convertibility to residents: of the total Fund membership, only 51 are listed as not having a current account and 31 as not having capital account restrictions (for resident-owned funds) as defined by the Fund according to Article VIII.   In other words, there are very few countries that allow convertibility for holders of their currency for nearly all transactions. But there are few, if any, countries that allow their currency to be converted on demand for any purpose a holder may wish to entertain.

Convertibility can be a powerful tool in the formulation and implementation of economic policy under proper conditions.   Because most East European commentators on the subject generally fail to specify all key parameters when they endorse the movement toward convertibility for local currencies and the transferable ruble, or both, such a policy stance may give rise to many legitimate, but not authoritative, interpretations.   This uncertainty is especially pronounced when, as at present, the objectives of ongoing policy discussions, feasible long-term policy goals, or emerging institutions are under comprehensive reassessment or are already in considerable flux.   To avoid erroneous evaluations, observers should not entertain unrealistic policy options for changing the model and development strategy of CPEs.   To affirm that convertibility for the ruble, forint, leu, or any other CPE currency is impossible is as meaningful as the converse.   There is indeed no structural or systemic impossibility to establishing some highly circumscribed form of convertibility by legal means (see Altman 1962, 367).

Moreover, the very concept of convertibility in the present configuration of the international monetary system is fundamentally ambiguous.   It was originally derived from the possibility of converting paper money into gold at a parity guaranteed by the emitting institution.   Under this regime, convertibility was universal, total, and predictable.   Especially since the demise in the early 1970s of the fixed exchange rate regime as the anchor of the monetary system established at Bretton Woods, convertibility has become restrained, partial, and indirect.   In view of these qualifications, it might perhaps be better to dispense with the term and replace it with "exchangeability" (Dunajewski 1979, 195), a term suggestive of one currency's ability to be turned into another on demand, subject to certain limitations. From now on, I shall use convertibility in that sense. An exegesis of the plausible variants of convertibility that have been envisaged by the CPEs may help to gauge the relevance and bearing of the analysis for intra-CMEA cooperation or the financing of East-West trade. It may also clarify the considerable misunderstanding in the literature about convertibility in CPEs individually and the CMEA as a whole.

Without going into a lengthy literature study, the key issues involved can best be grasped if the parameters of the concept are fully defined. An important consideration is the distinction between commodity and financial convertibility. Commodity convertibility allows the holder of a currency to purchase any desired good or service at the prevailing price in the currency's home market. This presupposes the existence of local markets that allow holders of that currency to purchase goods and services, including exports. Financial convertibility allows the holder of a currency to change it into any other at the prevailing exchange rate, a rate that could have been fixed previously by legal agreement or could have resulted from free or managed currency markets. This one variant gives rise to four combinations: financial and commodity inconvertibility; financial and commodity convertibility; financial convertibility but commodity inconvertibility; and financial inconvertibility but commodity convertibility.

A second consideration is whether financial or commodity convertibility, or possibly both, is envisaged for residents or nonresidents. This would imply seven possible combinations: financial and commodity convertibility for residents and nonresidents or for only one of these categories; financial and commodity inconvertibility for residents and nonresidents; financial convertibility and commodity inconvertibility for residents, nonresidents, or both; or financial inconvertibility and commodity convertibility for residents and nonresidents or for only one of these categories.

The third consideration is whether financial or commodity convertibility for either residents or nonresidents applies to all currency markets or only to some. This would yield 19 logical combinations if there are only two markets, that is, the "home country" and "abroad." The reader can readily grasp the combinations.

A last important consideration concerns the particular currency that is being envisaged for conversion. Given the segregated markets typical of the CMEA and its constituent economies, convertibility could be entertained for transactions by enterprises that now fall within the compass of regular transferable ruble commercial agreements, the domestic currency holdings of households, or the domestic enterprise or producer currency balances kept at the state bank. By my reckoning, this yields 127 logically different combinations. If convertibility were to be sought for some goods (for instance, consumer durables) but not for others, as was at one point under discussion in the CMEA and has recently been reintroduced (see Section V), there would be an even larger number of logical combinations.

Perhaps most important in assessing the portent of the convertibility debate is whether reference is to commodity convertibility, financial convertibility, or both. Most currencies of developed market economies are convertible in both senses. Experience has demonstrated, however, that some degree of financial convertibility has been easiest to introduce when a large measure of commodity convertibility had previously been attained. Historically, the convertibility for current account transactions has preceded that of capital flows to the extent that freely functioning capital markets have emerged at all. But this precedent deriving from the behavior and requirements of market economies need not apply universally.

The key features of the economic model of the CPEs and of their trade and payments regimes illustrate the different degrees of convertibility they have already achieved. Excepting periods of physical allocation and rationing, money held by resident consumers in these countries possesses a high degree of commodity convertibility. As a result, the greatest progress has been achieved in introducing some measure of financial convertibility for this consumer currency. Considerable progress has also been made for nonresidents. To maintain consumer market balance in the CPEs, however, some foreign exchange controls are obviously required to regulate spending by holders of other inconvertible currencies. Inadequately forecast spending sprees, and thus disruptions of domestic markets, are invariably associated with any "liberalization" of unorganized tourism (Brabant 1987a, 217-18).

On the other hand, money balances in the enterprise sphere are extremely inconvertible, especially in orthodox CPEs, both in the financial and in the commodity sense. Because economic resources are *de rigueur* distributed with the explicit approval of the relevant planning authorities, money cannot command goods and services within the enterprise sector of the traditional CPE. Goods inconvertibility prevails because the holder of a currency balance must generally pass through the planning hierarchy and obtain clearance prior to being granted title to mobilize the balance. East European currencies are, in principle, internally inconvertible into goods for transactions outside the consumer sphere because any producer with net bank balances can acquire inputs only with the explicit approval of the relevant planning authorities. If an enterprise commands a good, it is because it has been allocated by the plan, not because it has bank balances. Therefore, the plan is the motive behind the movement of resources. The associated money flows are merely an automatic response to prior decisions about the movement of resources. Just as it cannot purchase local goods, an enterprise with a money balance cannot normally acquire other currencies without first obtaining approval of the banking, trading, or central planning administration.

The possible degree of commodity convertibility will remain highly confined as long as the planner preempts the decision-making process by allocating goods directly rather than through some market. Internal commodity inconvertibility has been much relaxed in recent years, and one focal element of the ongoing reform debate is the scrapping of major components of the material-technical supply system in favor of wholesale trade ("direct enterprise relations" in current parlance). The CPEs that have taken a meaningful step in the direction of the devolution of decisionmaking have by necessity created some limited range for real markets. This also holds for nonresidents. Commodity and financial convertibility for nonresidents depends critically on the planning system in the CPEs. It has foundered thus far essentially because of the absence of domestic markets for producer goods and the limited discretion of enterprise managers to use money holdings.

Regarding the transferable ruble, it is important to recall that there is no central planning agency at the CMEA level and that regional trade and payments are regulated through various administrative channels of bargaining about quantities and prices of traded goods. There is thus some potential for the emergence of goods convertibility provided the negotiators involved can let quantities and prices move in step with shifts in the aggregate demand and supply of all participants. This has clearly not been the case to date, as is well known, because of price heterogeneity and the inability of negotiators to bargain chiefly on the basis of economic criteria. Bilateral trade and payments agreements stifle the potential for commodity convertibility in this sphere. Transferable ruble money balances are involuntary because, as noted, money as such does not command goods. The gradual emergence of the transferable ruble's financial convertibility will succeed without a hitch once CMEA trade prices can flexibly reflect the region's real demand and supply.

II. CONVERTIBILITY: BENEFITS AND COSTS

To maintain monetary and balance-of-payments equilibrium when the central plan is the paramount regulator of economic decisions, it may be far easier in a number of respects to achieve and to defend currency convertibility than is the case with a market economy. This proposition may sound paradoxical, but it is not. Given the enormous powers of central decisionmakers, for example, the CPE has the ability to defend domestic price stability and to minimize economic fluctuations provided it formulates its plans realistically and succeeds in having them carried out. As such, exchange rates are stable, and the state is in a position to plan balance-of-payments equilibrium. Neither can be endangered by speculation. Furthermore, the currency issue can be controlled strictly and need not be undermined by foreign capital flows in either direction as a result of the lack of monetary discipline, though such an environment does not necessarily create an economically meaningful form of convertibility.

Generally speaking, the power of convertibility to formulate and implement economic policy derives from the flexible access to

markets and hence its fostering of wider competition on the basis
of scarcity indicators. As such, it can contribute immeasurably to
maintaining the proper market signals for the home country, thus
ensuring efficient resource allocation. Although the CPEs have
been keenly aware of the broad advantages that could eventually be
reaped from a more flexible foreign exchange regime, policymakers thus far have not been overly preoccupied with the possible role
of convertibility in promoting more efficient resource allocation.
They have shown a keener interest in exploiting the advantages of
convertibility in formulating trade decisions and in using domestic resources in some sectors that remain quite isolated from the
rest of the economy. How this could be exploited and to what extent
these economies are prepared to modify their policies, institutions,
and policy instruments are, however, separate issues.

Decisionmakers in CPEs are well aware of the advantages of
convertibility, but they are also seriously concerned about its draw-
backs. This creates ambivalence arising in part because the "ideal
model" coveted by CPE planners is not yet well defined. Full convertibility may provide a highly useful institutional prop for a wide
range of policies if the economy permits smooth, even if not instantaneous, adjustments in quantities and prices. If macroeconomic managers aspire to something different, the most desirable
option is not necessarily full-fledged convertibility.

The advantages are normally perceived to be fourfold. First, a
convertible CPE currency would be accepted for trading purposes.
Foreign asset holders may also wish to accumulate some of their
funds in that currency in view of the stability and earning potential in CPEs (Kazandzieva 1983, 36). Favorable access to short- and
long-term capital in the form of, for example, loans, bonds, and
supplier credits may yield seigniorage to the emitting CPE.
However, in the postwar monetary evolution, only two vehicle currencies—chiefly, the dollar and pound sterling—may have benefited from seigniorage, and even this positive appraisal is being
questioned by some knowledgeable observers. Economic agents are
likely to hold CPE currency balances only for transaction purposes
and only if they can be turned into goods directly or indirectly.

Second, convertibility enables the issuer to encourage other countries to participate in the CMEA's multilateral settlements mechanism and capital markets, provided a transition toward real multi-

lateralism becomes feasible. Needless to say, in this the CPEs have been motivated more by concerns about obtaining flexible access to international commercial and financial markets than by considerations about granting advantageous conditions to third countries. Any geographical widening of the transferable ruble's use in regular commerce or in capital markets is crucially contingent on a transition toward real multilateralism linked to a gradual commitment to goods convertibility.

Third, currency convertibility makes for relatively flexible commercial relations in international markets because it implies multilateralism with all other convertible currency users. It also favorably affects the CPE's access to short- and long-term capital in the form of, for example, loans, bonds, and supplier credits. Furthermore, it permits transactions that are often precluded due to lack of adequate foreign exchange revenues. Although such advantages can be expected from the more general salutary implications of convertibility for the allocation process, the main emphasis in the CPE literature on the benefits of convertibility is not primarily on the determination of the level and commodity composition of trade, but rather on the geographical distribution of a predetermined trade volume.

Finally, convertibility calls for frequent reappraisal of the exchange rate. The latter's realism helps to maintain balance-of-payments equilibrium, serves as a real measure of value linking the external economy with world markets, and ensures a proper relationship between domestic prices and world market prices. Closely related to the exchange rate issue, but not necessarily identical to it in the CPE context, is the advantage of maintaining a proper relationship between domestic prices and world market prices for those countries that perceive such a nexus as an integral element of macroeconomic regulation (Kazandzieva 1983, 33). Note, however, that the advocates regard convertibility mainly as a convenient means of reaping higher trade gains, and not necessarily as a powerful instrument to refocus the development strategy of trade-dependent economies.

Convertibility is not, however, a one-way street. For an economy operating with real markets and subject to a minimum of control on the part of the authorities, the net effect of convertibility is likely to be positive. But its drawbacks may well outweigh the associated advantages for economies that exhibit pervasive administrative, controls, political interference in economic processes, and substantial economic imbalances. The most frequently cited arguments in favor of creating convertibility in the CPEs hinge on the feasibility of minimal economic reforms. Advocates regard convertibility mainly as a convenient means of reaping higher trade gains and a greater influx of foreign capital, but not necessarily as a powerful instrument to refocus the development strategy of trade-dependent economies and facilitate resource allocation. Disadvantages of convertibility, on the other hand, are identified in particular in the sphere of market-type relations. I will summarize six crucial disadvantages that have been most frequently discussed.

First, a convertible transferable ruble or local currency may become the object of speculation in international financial markets for sound economic reasons, but possibly also for political or strategic motives. Similarly, non-CPE firms and institutions may accumulate transferable ruble balances and then suddenly decide to convert them into goods or other currencies, thereby injecting an element of unwelcome volatility into the "stability" of CMEA currencies and the domestic economies. Because domestic stability remains one of the paramount objectives of socialist economic policies, the uncertainty engendered by convertibility raises the question of whether the CPEs would be able to neutralize such speculative pressures with their presently available economic resources.

Second, the freedom to convert currency balances into goods presupposes the abolition of essential components of trade planning and the monopoly of foreign trade. At the least, it could greatly weaken central control over trade and payments, a development that may manifest itself in two different forms. In the absence of credible macroeconomic monetary and fiscal policies, commodity convertibility is bound to weaken the monopoly of foreign trade. Once such aggregate domestic policies are firmly in place, however, the monopoly of foreign trade loses control over the details of day-to-day foreign exchange transactions, while its role as the center guiding microeconomic decisions rises perceptibly. The mere fact that such a disintegrating development might materialize has been taken as a pointer that free convertibility is incompatible with socialist socioeconomic precepts.   Especially with regard to price policies, negative consequences of a socialist currency entering capitalist markets have been identified with the monetary pressures on prices in market economies and their trade, and their possible transmission to the CPEs (Konstantinov 1983, 11).

Third, convertibility raises the issue of how to forestall and eliminate disequilibria in the regional or overall external payments balance.   The only lasting solution seems to be to seek fundamental adaptations in the surplus as well as in the deficit CPEs to cope with disequilibria that stem from structural dislocations.

Fourth, currency convertibility or even convertibility into goods requires the accumulation of adequate reserves.   There is no precise guideline on the exact magnitude of what is "adequate."   There is little doubt, however, that the CPEs must be prepared to accumulate more reserves than they have in the past to cushion balance-of-payments effects or to counter a run on their currency.   The accumulation of substantial reserves requires considerable investment. Such an allocation is deemed unattainable in the short run by most CPEs because of the already widespread payments pressures on their convertible currency trade. Furthermore, such a substantial "unproductive" investment has traditionally been viewed as an unwarranted appropriation of scarce investment funds that drains resources from more productive activities.   Even a temporary, if deliberate, growth deceleration to build up reserves would seem to be unacceptable to most policymakers.   This is particularly true at the current time, after nearly a decade of minimal growth in per capita incomes, and when there is an enormous backlog in claims on investment funds for modernization and to meet social needs.

Fifth, all types of currency convertibility require substantial administrative adaptations and most likely also changes in economic structures and policies.   Apart from these changes, which themselves could temporarily induce a substantial upswing in East-West trade, convertibility may divert economic relations in favor of market economies.   Any such substantial, permanent reorientation of commerce away from the CMEA is presumed to be detrimental to socialist economic integration by all those keenly interested in bolstering this regional cohesion as one platform for consolidating regional power, not necessarily in the economic field.   It is also doubtful that such commercial reorientation could take place without the CPE incurring marked terms-of-trade losses if they were to obtain such wide access to market economy trade.

Finally, the willingness of agents in market economies to hold CPE currencies—any other direction of the monetary flows would not directly benefit the CPEs—clearly depends on trade prospects, the room for direct foreign investments in the CPEs, and, to some extent, on what such funds earn in socialist banks. Currency convertibility necessarily calls for changes in the regional and domestic credit and interest rate policies of the CPEs, changes East European commentators traditionally presume to be counterproductive. This view is held in particular by CPEs that still hope to benefit from low-cost loans from socialist partners.

III. SCHOOLS OF THOUGHT ON CONVERTIBILITY

Three positions on convertibility appear to hold sway at this stage. Perhaps the most radical position contends that one big shock would create the conditions necessary to a convertible currency, at least for wholesale trade. Certainly, unleashing all the economic forces that will force a new equilibrium may bring about the conditions necessary for sustaining a convertible currency. The question really is whether the forces to be released will be acceptable to society and lead to a new balance reflecting sociopolitical preferences. I do not presently perceive any CPE, let alone the CMEA as a whole, to be prepared politically or organizationally to enact any such shock short of a full-scale revolution, a revolution that would, by definition, eliminate the problem the country is trying to resolve. I believe this would hold even if outside resources were available to support such a movement.

Without active efforts on the part of all reforming CPEs to "harden" from within the CMEA their capacity to gain a more competitive position in world markets, in my view the costs of such a shock in terms of socioeconomic adjustment are bound to be horrendous. If so, it is most likely to prove unacceptable from a sociopolitical point of view. Although remarkable changes in the climate in which such deliberations occur have been crystallizing over the past years, the fragile social, political, and economic frameworks cannot survive sharp cuts in the standards of living in a comparatively short period, although there is a weak precedent. Vietnam liberalized its domestic markets and prices in early 1989, including the convertible currency exchange rate, but these changes are not sufficient to make the dong convertible.

Similarly, I find the economic reasoning behind recommendations to achieve convertibility through currency auctions or similar currency allocation schemes highly flawed. By definition, this is not convertibility in its usual sense. Such schemes can be justified only if they are applied in the context of genuine markets in which one class of currency holders (for example, resident enterprises) can trade excess currency balances acquired under truly competitive conditions. Without this condition, enterprises may be inclined to sell currency that is not earned in a profitable way at a rate that, certainly from the point of view of social profitability, is too low to be acceptable. In fact, in a situation with a considerable monetary overhang, as prevails in most reforming CPEs, enterprises flush with local currency may bid up the price of foreign currency, obtaining profits only because of prevailing irrational prices and rationing of goods in resource allocation mechanisms.

Finally, some convertibility advocates consider it simply a means of encouraging western investors and financiers to pour new money into East Europe. Certainly, convertibility may bring such a public-relations benefit in the short run. As East Europe's enormous debt and the weak response to ever laxer regulations on foreign investment (even in Vietnam, where they are very permissive indeed) demonstrate, the key problem in attracting foreign capital is that these countries compete in a global market for the distribution of excess savings. Such capital flows are motivated more by profits and the ability to incorporate local profits in the global allocation of resources (that is, potential convertibility) of transnational corporations than by the possibility of having convertibility per se imposed upon the currently highly regulated socialist economy. Surely, profits from joint ventures can be covered through convertible currency earnings of the CPE directly. This can also be done indirectly through an imaginative countertrade or compensatory trade arrangement.

IV. THE STARTING CONDITIONS FOR ECONOMIC REFORM

Examining the trade and payments regimes of a traditional CPE, and how it has attempted to accommodate its typical national conditions onto the CMEA platform, illuminates what is required to create gradually the preconditions for reaching and making use of a convertible currency. Identifying the key peculiarities of the evolution of these regimes will suffice for the purposes of identifying the existing attitude regarding the gradual move toward a more convertible regime (for a detailed examination of this issue, see Brabant 1987a, 1987b, and 1989a).

National Trade and Payments Regimes

These logically follow from the way CPE policymakers conceived their orthodox economic model and development strategy, and from the legacies thereof in various reform attempts undertaken since the late 1950s. The development strategy strives to achieve full employment, rapid socioeconomic growth, extensive industrialization, and a substantial degree of domestic policy autonomy to support elaboration of a more or less autarkic economic mechanism. For most of the postwar period, this development strategy sprang from the prototype economic model borrowed from the Soviet Union, which consisted of institutions, microeconomic and macroeconomic behavioral rules and policies, and policy instruments designed to implement forced industrialization. Dominated by hierarchical planning and management anchored to normative behavioral prescriptions, decisionmaking authority was vested at the center of national power to ensure a close link between political and economic functions.

Because central planning in physical detail usurps the role of orthodox macroeconomic and microeconomic policies, most economic decisions are channeled through a complex, fairly bureaucratic administrative hierarchy in which economic considerations are only one set of issues motivating planners and ministerial bureaucrats, not to mention trade union and party interest groups.

Integral to this CPE model is the more or less complete separation of the domestic economy from external influences by means of special instruments and institutions. Foreign trade decisions are formulated through the central planning process and its associated institutions and instruments rather than through decisions formed on the basis of real microeconomic scarcity indicators. As a result, external economic relations are not an articulated component of the CPE. Trade levels tend to be well below what is considered "normal" for countries of similar size and at a similar level of development. There are, in addition, biases in the commodity composition and geographical distribution of trade compared with what would prevail in a market environment.

The organizational disjunction between the domestic economy and foreign economic activities has been accomplished by creation of a state monopoly of foreign trade and payments consisting of various organizational and financial ministerial levels as well as separate foreign trade organizations. The latter purchase domestic products destined for export and sell earmarked imports at domestic fiat prices. Differences between domestic and foreign prices converted at the official or commercial exchange rate, both of which are arbitrarily determined, are offset by the so-called price-equalization account, which is a component of the central government budget usually managed by the central bank as monobank. The monopoly of foreign trade, in my view, also involves total control of central agencies over strategic trade and foreign exchange decisionmaking, including making commercial policy and deciding strategic directions for development. These two aspects are rarely separated in analyses of CPE reforms, probably because they tend to collapse into one sphere only in the traditional CPE. In my estimate, however, such a logical distinction is required to avoid simplistic statements and bland generalizations about the abolition of the monopoly of foreign trade by policy design or its mortal erosion as a result of the impact of the ongoing economic reforms. If the monopoly of foreign trade is understood to include the second component as well, I cannot see its disintegration being considered in most CPEs. This has important implications for convertibility and a number of issues related to economic policy and regional economic integration.

Because trade by definition eludes the complete control of one planning center, the CPEs attempt to gain greater stability in the domestic economy by forecasting trade flows as accurately as possi-

ble. This is usually accomplished in the context of detailed bilateral trade and payments agreements constructed around relatively
stable, if artificial, prices. These apply in particular to trade among
CPEs, for which a special transferable ruble price regime emerges
(Brabant 1987b), and among CPEs with some developing countries
with whom clearing arrangements are maintained. These organizational accommodations are one determinant of the geographical bias in the trade orientation of CPEs. Because money plays a
minimal role, key features of the CPE's trade model include: multiple exchange rates reflecting multi-tier domestic price systems;
currency and commodity inconvertibility complementing planned
resource allocation; bilateralism facilitating the planned conduct of
foreign trade; and exchange controls insulating domestic from
foreign markets.

In this standard CPE model, macroeconomic decisionmakers
and especially enterprise managers are poorly informed about the
real economic cost of their import-substitution policies, in large
part because they remain physically removed from trading markets. When growth slows, central planners naturally seek relief
by increasingly enmeshing the economy in foreign·economic relations as a pivotal prop for domestic growth. To confront the multiple opportunities in domestic and foreign trade sectors, policymakers begin to explore new decision criteria and organizational
forms to stimulate more efficient trade relations. But they do not
completely abandon autonomous economic policies. Thus, the link
between domestic and foreign prices remains highly tenuous and
discreet; and pseudo exchange rates (called currency coefficients,
multipliers, reproduction coefficients, transaction rates, and so on)
are just that: poor substitutes for an effective exchange rate.

Only when the CPE moves to comprehensive decentralization
can a different environment emerge. Countries coveting this status
in the first instance have been Vietnam and the Soviet Union, as
well as several East European CPEs (Bulgaria, Czechoslovakia,
Hungary, and Poland, the latter two having made noticeable
progress) and, of course, China (Mongolia to a far lesser extent).
In these CPEs, sweeping changes occurred in the foreign trade
sphere, largely paralleling those sought for domestic economic
agents.   These changes are more radical in countries like
Mongolia, the Soviet Union, and Vietnam than in other CPEs,

largely because the smaller East European countries had already introduced seminal changes in the organization and decision-making means of foreign trade in the early 1960s. Though the reforms within which these changes matured were aborted or sharply slowed down around 1970, the modifications in foreign trade sectors were on the whole maintained and, in many cases, further streamlined administratively in the 1970s and early 1980s.

Because of comprehensive marketization's effects, foreign trade organizations are now being transformed into effective self-accounting firms or their tasks are being assigned to private, cooperative, and state-owned production units that are self-accounting and self-financing. This requires markedly different managerial behavior from that which had prevailed in any of the other economic models tried by CPEs. Especially in the smaller countries, this altered behavior must emerge partly in response to the link between domestic and foreign prices through a realistic exchange rate. Because of the absence of genuine CMEA reform, the dichotomy between the latter and East-West markets remains a serious obstacle to effective reform, especially in the smaller CPEs that significantly depend on external commerce.

In convertible currency transactions, CPE firms are usually permitted to participate autonomously to the extent that foreign exchange can be earned from exports and made available for imports, possibly through licensing and currency auctions. But this does not hold for clearing currency trade, particularly within the CMEA framework. The small and isolated reforming CPE, such as Hungary was for many years, had little choice but to buffer domestic pricing and decisionmaking against CMEA currency and trade operations that could not be reconciled with the reform's objectives.

The CMEA Trade and Payments Regimes

The desire for close economic ties among the CPEs, particularly in East Europe after World War II, motivated these countries to create an international regime to support among other things their domestic objectives. The CMEA trade and payments regimes evolved largely in response to the expressed needs of the participants to pursue their own development interests through inward-oriented behavior. Within this sheltered CMEA environment, rules for trading and payments were instituted that differed markedly from those prevailing elsewhere. Economic cooperation within the CMEA was regulated mainly through fairly detailed bilateral trade and payments agreements forming a constituent part of domestic planning of the various member economies rather than of an agreed CMEA-wide policy.

The CMEA trade and payments regimes consist of the following features: formal multilateral settlements of bilateral payments imbalances by using the transferable ruble as the accounting unit, but keeping bilateral accounting of real trade flows intact; creation of the transferable ruble, establishment of nominally multilateral settlements procedures, and management of short-term credit at the International Bank for Economic Cooperation while maintaining the caesura between money and commodity transactions; coordination of investment intentions and promotion of joint investment financing through the International Investment Bank; introduction of the transferable ruble price regime into CMEA trade that is relatively autonomous and stable through the plan period, although actual transaction prices are set bilaterally, almost on an ad hoc basis; elaboration of a multiple exchange rate regime for various types of transactions that are, at best, poorly interlinked; and establishment of regional economic organizations, chiefly to facilitate the coordination of decisions between production and science, as well as of other fields considering technological progress. The CMEA mechanism as it has matured does not, however, embody a clear-cut set of macroeconomic policies for the region as a whole. Moreover, none of the aforementioned links of the CMEA economic mechanism has ever operated automatically. Because of the centrality of bilateral trade and payments agreements, economic cooperation can only be fostered within the context of concrete bilateral intergovernmental arrangements, including these agreements and variants of them. In some cases, certainly, individual firms of CPEs cooperate directly without the intermediation of the monopoly of foreign trade, although these activities develop only when the monopoly explicitly arranges for such links to emerge.

Strikingly, this passivity of the CMEA remained intact in spite of national and regional reform attempts, the recent economic

crises occurring especially in East Europe, the malaise about socialist economic integration since the mid-1970s, and general misgivings about the contribution of integration to economic growth in
the CPEs. It is only since late 1987 that signs of change have been
emerging, three of which are relevant to the theme of this article:
(1) the redrawing of the role of planning in fostering socialist
economic integration; (2) the enactment of an integration strategy
that in time should lead to a common market; and (3) the transformation of a cooperation mechanism (policies, institutions, and
instruments) that will give priority to economics and interfirm relations in determining CMEA cooperation. These developments
are, of course, directly related to reforms being enacted in key
CPEs, first and foremost the Soviet Union.

It is important to emphasize that these reforms are desired and
that the incipient changes are only the first building blocks toward
effective marketization within any of the CPEs and *a fortiori* within
the CMEA as a whole.

V. NATIONAL AND REGIONAL REFORM

Perhaps the key reason for the pro-reform sentiment in virtually
all CMEA members has been the growth difficulties encountered
in the early 1980s. With little scope to accelerate growth from factor supply or redistribution (Brabant 1987c), most CPEs must seek
productivity gains by creating room for policy maneuvers. This is
to some degree a function of proper incentives to sensitize the development environment to the preconditions of factor productivity
growth. Aggregate economic policies, institutions, and behavioral
rules are especially important for dovetailing the decisions of economic agents with economy-wide ambitions. These measures
should emerge primarily from indirect coordination instruments
and supporting institutions through monetary, fiscal, price, and income policies. Improved economic performance through shifts in
the methods and goals of national and regional economic policies
is critical in this regard. Of course, these include the more
coherent linking of domestic and foreign economic activities.

Critical areas of the reform focus on attaining greater autonomy
and economic self-support in the microeconomic sphere, both of

which are contingent on the realization of genuine competition and realistic price formation. If the enterprise has no control over input or output prices and, hence, adjustments in demand and supply, its own profitability criterion is likely to differ palpably from that which is appropriate for the economy as a whole. Even financial autonomy predicated on the enactment of an efficient banking sector and a revamped fiscal system is unlikely to be very helpful in this regard. Especially important is the centrality of prices and foreign trade and payments regimes.

Although price reform is perhaps the most pivotal reform element, it is also arguably the most complex and politically sensitive task, one that has undone reforms and reformers on more than one occasion. Price reform is a daunting task, but policymakers have found it increasingly counterproductive and financially very taxing to maintain domestic price distortions through large consumer price subsidies, to avoid passing on the basic changes in trade prices, and to command production and consumption decisions through physical allocations. In other words, circumstances have compelled nearly all CPEs to reevaluate their pronounced preference for price stability. As a result, the erstwhile predictability of constant retail and inflexible wholesale prices, with changes introduced on a comprehensive basis only after long intervals, has been considerably lessened during the past decade. But price movements have varied in a noticeably differentiated pattern depending on the country and the type of goods. Its various aspects can be discussed in three ways: (1) in terms of price level and structures, and the relationship among various domestic price tiers and between domestic and foreign trade prices; (2) in terms of the desired speed of price adjustment; (3) and in terms of the comprehensiveness of the reform and the levels at which it should be undertaken (Petrakov 1987). Among the measures envisaged, the linking of trade and domestic prices is critical; hence, the realistic exchange rate or a surrogate in the form, for example, of a multiplier, commercial exchange rate, internal exchange rate, or reproduction coefficient (Brabant 1987a, 198-207). Countries have rarely tried to let the exchange rate find its own equilibrium, with price adjustments undertaken in line with the government's pricing policy. The only exception known to me is Vietnam, which in early 1989, after a decade of off and on decentralization reforms, simply decided to engage the market head-on and let all but a few prices (basically electrical energy and transportation) be determined by supply and demand, albeit with significant and at times ill-advised government interference.

Instead of maintaining the foreign trade and payments regime as a key support of domestic policy autonomy, most reforms seek to entrust greater responsibility, including self-financing, to individual firms. In terms of behavioral requirements, this is quite a different environment from the one in which foreign trade organizations are kept afloat through price-equalization applied to the strict provisions of bilateral trade and payments agreements as in the case of clearing trade and central prescriptions for trade with hard currency partners.

Just as important for effective economic decentralization as the judicious introduction of indirect coordination instruments and their associated policy institutions are appropriate macroeconomic policies within proper policy institutions equipped with instruments adequate for the purpose they are to serve. These policies must support and fine tune the policy instruments, and, indeed, guide economic units in raising efficiency. Another task of macroeconomic policy, which is the central role of statewide planning, is structural change and the revamping of growth strategies, for example, through large-scale investment projects. Finally, central planning and macroeconomic policy must maintain control over the so-called nonmaterial sphere, that is, all activities that are either quintessentially socialist in nature, including education, medical care, the arts, and the basic infrastructure, or are typically reserved for governmental action, for example, defense.

With regard to the economic sphere, key macroeconomic policies that are traditionally very primitive in the classical CPE include monetary, fiscal, and income policies due to ideological precepts and especially to the primacy of quantitative planning. Monetary policy must be activated and extended to many new economic activities to provide macroeconomic stability, to let the central bank act as the effective lender of last resort for decentralized financial institutions, to regulate absorption in line with available domestic and borrowed resources, and to supervise a greater diversity of assets available to currency holders that must be innovated in an increasingly autonomous, decentralized financial structure.

The latter can be created without necessarily encroaching on the socialist ideology regarding property (see Nuti 1989).

Inasmuch as the CMEA is the key market of the CPEs, what a country in isolation can achieve significantly depends on the degree to which CMEA conditions differ from those of world markets and indeed from the aspirations of the individual country. Improved economic performance through shifts in the methods and goals of economic policies in the CMEA context is critical in this regard. The CMEA's system-specific policies, institutions, and instruments are not well geared toward supporting reform measures spontaneously. What role, then, can be assigned to the CMEA as a regional economic institution, a forum for experimentation, and a regional "market" in support of as yet unsynchronized reform attempts? Should the CMEA be envisaged as a buttress to the CPEs embarking on ambitious reforms, while protecting those that choose to move more slowly? Alternatively, should the changes be targeted at supporting chiefly the greatest common denominator of various members' economic mechanisms and at incorporating at the regional level some features of the most conservative reform?

Although many legacies from 40 years of CMEA cooperation are bound to impinge upon the CMEA's perestroika, how this will happen is a question that cannot be answered adequately because we know only the rough contours of the proposed changes that are presently gaining support and approval from the key members. It may be useful, therefore, to study the desirable modifications of cooperation modes, the extent to which prevailing conditions are sufficiently mature to facilitate the swift realization of these intentions, and the conditions that must be fulfilled for these envisioned transformations to materialize. I assume that key CMEA members will continue with reforms and that there is no ready alternative to emphasizing economic integration as a prime source of growth in CPEs, at least until countries succeed in restoring domestic and external balance in their economies to a level and structure of activity that will enhance their competitiveness in the world economy.

Since the early 1980s, there has been considerable agitation for reversing the passivity of the CMEA. This has been manifested by efforts in three areas: (1) the revamping of the institutional set-up of the CMEA with a view to rationalizing the bureaucracy, streamlining the mechanisms through which issues get tabled, and rendering the deliberative organs more effective; (2) the reexamining of the purposes of socialist economic integration, the supporting institutions, and the instruments at the disposal of agents to coordinate structural macroeconomic policies; and (3) the refocusing of the institutions and instruments of economic integration, which includes providing effective support for emerging reforms. As a result of these efforts and the critical examination they have generated at all levels, five groups of issues can be distinguished.

Perhaps the most important elements of CMEA's perestroika are the elaboration of a new socialist economic integration strategy, entitled "Collective Concept of the International Socialist Division of Labor for the Period 1991-2005," and a sharp revision in the economic mechanism that is to support this strategy. The CPEs now aim to move beyond previous plans and programs for integrating the region by taking a fresh look at the objectives, policies, instruments, and basic institutional supports of regional cooperation. This new policy was endorsed in Prague in 1988, but further refinements were to be readied in time for the 40th anniversary celebrations in 1989, culminating in the June 1989 summer session in Sofia, after a third summit of the 1980s set for Prague in March 1989. The latter was postponed until April and later until May, only to be scrapped altogether because of serious disagreements. The regular session was postponed until October at the earliest.[1]

Although the common market idea was endorsed as a long-term aim—and even that with Romania's dissent—as have been virtually all previous attempts to bolster socialist economic integration, I believe greater urgency to do something positive and bold now exists. The pressure to act has built up too long, and economic crises cannot be eliminated without decisive action toward genuine integration in regional and global economic affairs. Export-led growth at this stage of lingering internal and external imbalances in these countries depends critically on making a quantum leap in regional economic integration while regaining lost ground in world markets. However, this must proceed slowly. Such a step forward requires unorthodox, imaginative initiatives

1. *Magyar Hírlap,* June 27, 1989, p. 5.

that motivate economic agents by bolstering their material and other interest in integration matters. Hence the emphasis on opening up capital, labor, and goods markets to reestablish faster growth. Concrete details on how the unified market may develop are unknown, but evidently genuine commercial policy will emerge that may include a customs union and later a common market. Needless to say, many critical issues continue to form the ongoing policy agenda for deliberation and policy action. Convertibility is only one of the items, and certainly not the most urgent one at this juncture.

Directly related to the program are major decisions revolving around the precise nature of the socialist economic integration mechanism to be elaborated in conjunction with, and perhaps in support of, the ongoing reform process in key CPEs. Gaining concurrence on this matter has been much more problematical. Although there was broad agreement in Moscow on the need to revisit key elements of the traditional forms of regional cooperation through planning and to overhaul the passive monetary-financial instruments and institutions at hand into innovative ones, members were divided on a number of critical economic issues. These included the introduction of a modified, highly limited form of regional convertibility, multilateralism in trade and payments through the International Bank for Economic Cooperation, the determination of unified exchange rates, the revision of the transferable ruble price-formation mechanism, the linking of domestic and trade prices, and the enhancing of CMEA capital movements through the International Investment Bank's credit mechanism. Special emphasis has been on improving the organizational prerequisites, the institutional supports, the macroeconomic policy environment and formulation, and the economic instruments that allow firms from different countries to interact directly, including with regard to decisions concerning the determination of prices and output. These and other elements of the refurbished mechanism in support of socialist economic integration must be in place in time for the introduction of the next medium-term plans in 1991. An unusual item on the agenda is the creation of socialist multinationals centered around key national firms (Shiryaev 1989).

VI. MOVING TOWARD CONVERTIBILITY

If the foregoing is an accurate assessment of the current ferment surrounding socialist economic integration, expectations are very high. But before they can be realized, key policies regarding the non-European CMEA members and the new socialist economic integration concept must be further refined. Perhaps most important is the reconstruction of the integration mechanism by 1990 and the new thinking about prices, direct wholesale trade, exchange rates, convertibility, capital movements, and regional settlements. Although there is undoubtedly reason for guarded optimism concerning the prospects for meaningful change in the economic integration mechanism, past experiences indicate it would be premature to expect swift progress. If the vanguard CPEs can accept the notion of rebuilding the integration mechanism by allowing countries to follow different, though synchronized, integration tracks in accordance with agreed-upon modalities, the prospects of regional economic integration will brighten considerably.

As the definitions in Section I indicate, convertibility as a means to gear resource allocation is inalienably linked to the existence of fairly integrated markets in which economic agents operate with a great degree of discretion, subject to the overall rules of the game set by, and ensured mainly through, monetary and fiscal policies. At least in my view, convertibility is by definition a category that makes sense only when it is associated with the automatic and anonymous clearing of all or some classes of transactions. For that, it is necessary to create the fundamental preconditions. That is, it is unreasonable to approach convertibility through a support scheme when the preconditions for maintaining access to some markets in an anonymous and automatic fashion are not yet in place. This is *a fortiori* the case when there is no policy agreement on what can realistically be done, particularly with reference to price flexibility and competition through genuine wholesale trade markets. In my view, those conditions can only be created by the countries that believe they suffer from inconvertibility. Measures must be embraced by CMEA countries individually or as a group, perhaps with some outside support as a palliative. I still believe that the latter is a more realistic and promising alternative than anything else I have seen in the recent literature.

Much has been written in recent years about the further improvement of the transferable ruble as an international currency and its associated settlements mechanism, including the possibility of a gradual transition to convertibility. Similar speculation about local currencies has been made on a number of occasions. This was particularly pronounced in connection with the Integration Program. Although some of these measures were introduced in the 1970s, it was in a highly perfunctory manner with the result that they had little if any impact on commercial relations in the CMEA (Brabant 1989c; Válek 1985, 11). Inasmuch as the political will toward progress has always been absent, one may well question whether this backdrop is a harbinger of what may presently be under discussion. If so, why is the issue of convertibility emerging again?

However, key elements of a market environment are not yet present in CPEs. This pertains especially to the establishment of genuine wholesale trade and flexible prices. Their realization as a rule requires time and perseverance to cushion the adverse socio-economic effects of the necessary adjustments. Moreover, wholesale and retail markets are far from integrated. Of course, trade markets themselves are hardly homogeneous, given transferable ruble prices that are incompatible with world market prices, making the emergence of a convertible currency appear a realistic expectation only after a protracted transition phase. This is necessary first and foremost to bring about genuine markets with flexible prices and is needed even more to link these domestic markets to the global economy or its major components. The length of the transition period will depend on the ability and determination of the leaders to foster the kinds of reforms that will lead to the coveted objective.

A convertible currency can be sustained if the authorities are in a position to maintain approximate current account equilibrium with the reserves on hand, as well as loans that can be readily obtained from abroad and serviced. That is, the demand for and the supply of foreign exchange must balance at least over the medium term. If foreign exchange is traded through means other than markets, external convertibility can be guaranteed, but the country loses the critical contribution of such an instrument to enhance the efficiency of domestic and foreign resource allocation. For that to emerge, economic agents must be in a position to acquire and dispose of foreign exchange in a predictable manner. In other words, there must be a genuine foreign exchange market, which in turn is linked to competitive markets for goods and services throughout the economy. Whether or not effective aggregate demand and supply include a trade component, they should emerge from independent allocative decisions, not from a heavily constrained resource allocation mode.

The introduction of a full-fledged convertible currency in the CMEA region or in individual CPEs makes sense only if certain minimum conditions are fulfilled. Obviously, there must be adequate convertible currency reserves to cover any unexpected demand for foreign exchange. Moreover, economic growth must be ensured and yet yield an appropriate amount of competitive exportables. Perhaps foremost, the foreign exchange and trade regimes must be more flexible to take advantage of the demands of a convertible currency and to implement changes in the domestic economy in response to shifts in the demand and supply of the CPE's currency. It would be particularly useful to entrust current trade decisions to economic agents and to establish a direct link between domestic and trade prices, after "removal" of the monetary overhang, of course, to bridge the chasm between CMEA and world prices. Also, exchange rates that help reach and maintain balance-of-payments equilibrium must be set. Given the discrepancies between domestic scarcity relationships and what prevails elsewhere in the CMEA and, even more so, in world markets, goods convertibility is not likely to become a practical objective soon. This is the case even if policymakers remain committed to a reform course that envisages much greater latitude for indirect economic coordination. At the very least, a two-track course must be charted.

Convertibility in East-West Relations: A Transition

To serve the needs of the ongoing reform process, promoting convertibility in East-West relations must build on existing arrangements. Inasmuch as East-West trade is mainly conducted in convertible currencies, convertibility must be fostered primarily as a guide in resource allocation. This is particularly so if CPEs are genuinely interested in enhancing the scope of enterprise decisionmaking and directly linking domestic with foreign relations.

Convertibility in East-West relations initially should be envisaged for an enterprise's current account transactions. That is, movement toward convertibility should be based on an ever-growing efficient currency allocation scheme that eventually encompasses all foreign transactions by enterprises. For this process to foster proper choices, however, firms must have much greater price- and quantity-setting latitude. That is, the state must be prepared to confront price reform and genuine wholesale trade.

There are three obstacles to convertibility: (1) the monetary overhang from past imbalances; (2) incorrect relative prices; and (3) an unbalanced economic situation. Although in practice these three obstacles are difficult to disentangle, it is crucial to do so in policy approaches. Identification of the causes of the problem will facilitate the choice of the instrument and the corrective policy. Thus, past imbalances must be resolved through some mechanism that neutralizes or diverts the excess money in circulation. Unless the monetary overhang is significantly compressed, pursuing price reform to improve the decisionmaking criteria for economic agents will probably be hopeless. The current economic situation is primarily a matter of macroeconomic policy that should increasingly be placed under control of orthodox monetary and fiscal policies, perhaps augmented in the case of a socialist economy with price and incomes policies. Changing relative prices, however, should result from competition among and between businesses and households.

Once a solution to the accumulated imbalances is found, policymakers should consider a sharp devaluation of the currency in terms of, say, the dollar. This would ease external pressures in the medium to long run, but it might exacerbate short-term problems, particularly in the highly indebted CPEs. Next, allocating convertible currency through a more transparent mechanism than the largely administrative distribution modalities embraced so far should be found. Currency retention schemes are a possibility, but I do not find them very attractive. If foreign currency earned is more valuable than the price authorities place on it, the latter should be adjusted, as opposed to the former being rationed.

That is not to say that auctions are useless. Indeed, I would favor auction schemes, on a trial basis initially (for example, for categories of goods whose relative prices are not too distorted), and gradually for the bulk of foreign exchange. These auction markets must be carefully monitored at their inception in view of current imbalances, assuming that the inherited ones are somehow neutralized, and that relative prices are still far from market-clearing, thus distorting demand and supply of that currency. It is essential that most domestic and foreign prices of traded goods be linked, perhaps by some temporary buffers easing the adjustment process.

Such instruments should as much as possible come from commercial policy and be as nondiscretionary and transparent as circumstances permit. Until the link between domestic and foreign prices can be ensured chiefly through a flexible exchange rate and customs duties, the transition phase must be accompanied by other commercial policy arrangements (such as quotas on imports and perhaps on exports, subsidies, negotiated trade restraints), government measures to bolster entrepreneurial activity in foreign markets, and the buffering of nonconforming CMEA relations. It is important that such steps be taken not as a substitute for reform, but as a means of keeping the reform on track and reinforcing its momentum.

In addition, there is room for macroeconomic policymakers to ease the adjustment process. For example, most firms in CPEs that have strongly insulated their domestic markets are inexperienced in trading abroad. The government should expedite the learning process by easing the transfer of knowledge, for example, from the erstwhile foreign trade organizations to individual firms.

Regarding CMEA relations, I can see only one viable solution. If a CPE is genuinely interested in linking its economy with global markets, it must buffer this link against the "wrong" signals emanating from within CMEA relations. In the near future, trade with the CMEA group in general and the reforming CPEs in particular will continue to be heavily circumscribed by the involvement of central authorities. That is, intergovernmental agreements will establish the framework within which concrete trade quotas, sometimes for specific commodities, are to be decided. These must be accommodated as much as possible by each reforming economy separately. Moreover, the ongoing reforms probably will reduce the share of the centrally decided commitments in favor of ever-increasing room for firms themselves to negotiate over the quantities to be delivered and the terms of delivery. The government would essentially be responsible for the clearing of such transactions at realistic exchange rates.

There is no perfect solution to bridging the gap between CMEA and East-West economic relations as long as this divergence is supported in the real sphere. Measures to counter the problem must, therefore, be drawn up in a very pragmatic fashion. Reforming CPEs could take effective measures to accommodate prevailing CMEA peculiarities and take advantage of emerging relaxations, regardless of unequal levels of reform intentions. If economic renewal is to lead to integrated markets, the authorities themselves must decide how to come to grips with the peculiarities of the foreign exchange and commercial policies typical of the CMEA in comparison to features of world markets that the CPE desires to emulate. They can accomplish this through various means. One useful way of minimizing the degree of external dichotomy and its repercussions on the microeconomy is by buffering against transferable ruble prices at the border, that is, in effect levying ex post taxes and subsidies to equate prices of goods imported from and exported to the ruble area with domestic prices. In turn, domestic prices will be increasingly influenced by conditions in world markets. It is then up to the governments to decide whether the apparent costs and benefits of trading with the CMEA should be sustained or gradually diminished in favor of market orientation. Central authorities called on to negotiate bilateral trade and payments agreements with CMEA members should increasingly represent the interests of domestic firms in obtaining and disposing of some goods at prices that render microeconomic operations profitable.

At the same time, the reforming CPEs should bolster direct trade negotiations, including prices, among their own firms, which will increasingly be placed on a commercial footing. The issues of settling imbalances and introducing proper exchange rates to guide this behavior must be dealt with at the government level. There are now greater opportunities to make bulk quota commitments that can be cleared in different fashions from the orthodox transferable ruble price mechanism. This may be the necessary first step to initiating a movement toward currency convertibility in CMEA relations.

In other words, active state policy to foster relative price changes, including for foreign currency, through competition and genuine wholesale trade should in time enable the economy to sustain adjustments between demand and supply for its currency through market forces. At a later stage, the authorities may envisage loosening up the foreign currency markets for other transactors, including physical residents and nonresidents.

Convertibility in CMEA Relations: A Proposal

Convertibility in the CMEA is a much more complex issue. First, there is no single authority in place that can act according to the guidelines framed above to free up East-West economic relations. It is not even certain at this stage precisely what the majority view in the CMEA may be and to what degree that majority may be determined to pursue its ambitions, if necessary by leaving other CMEA participants behind. In addition to the problems that beset East-West economic relations, bilateralism and structural bilateralism in the CMEA impinge on the movement toward convertibility, making markets even less transparent than in the East-West case. As I have argued elsewhere (Brabant 1987a, 358-61), before meaningful progress can be made toward convertibility in the CMEA, it is necessary to ensure multilateralism and transferability. However, this does not mean that no progress can be made toward convertibility while at the same time ensuring greater multilateralism and transferability in CMEA trade.

It may be useful to consider two alternative paths. One is constructed around a European Payments Union-like strategy toward transferability that will lead directly to convertibility. The other is feasible with much more marketization, and it hinges on the degree of genuine price flexibility and competitive wholesale trade that CMEA countries are willing to pursue, including in their reciprocal economic relations.

A bold approach to laying the foundations of convertibility simply imposes it upon the region. All traders, whether state agencies or decentralized firms, would engage in transactions in local currency. Their negotiated prices would be geared to prevailing world market prices translated into local currency using the exchange rates set in open currency markets. In the latter markets, firms would obtain the transaction currency they require by competitively bidding on foreign exchange markets. Any imbalances sustained could be paid for in any currency, including convertible currency.

I believe that such a proposal puts the cart before the horse. It simply argues that if the CPEs are willing and able to place their CMEA relations on roughly the same footing as world markets and in addition make progress toward flexible domestic prices and competitive wholesale trading, they will achieve convertibility. Of course, such a conclusion is a truism.

An alternative, and in my view more realistic, scheme builds upon prevailing conditions and reform sentiments. Especially since mid-1985, the CPEs have stressed the advantages of genuine production specialization as the force behind regional economic integration. For this to succeed, particularly in parts and components in manufacturing, direct contacts among firms in production, distribution, technological development, or simple coordination of activities are a minimum requirement. The critical role of direct enterprise relations in fostering such specialization has recently been stressed in connection with the implementation of the program on Scientific-technological Progress. Since then, the debate on the scope and role of such relations in economic reforms in general and in encouraging socialist economic integration in particular has been lively. Where precisely this debate may lead is anybody's guess. I have the impression that Scientific-technological Progress is still a fashionable slogan. At least the results of efforts to enact direct enterprise relations, not just those coming under the above-cited program, have been very meager at best.

If direct enterprise relations, particularly in manufacturing, are to become the mainstay of regional economic integration, it would be counterproductive to seek balanced exchange in each and every interenterprise contract, which would amount to a further balkanization of structural bilateralism. Critical parameters that bear on such relations are regional pricing (including price-accounting rules and linkages among different price spheres), the smooth settlement of accounts, and harmonization of regional exchange rates. Regional "convertibility" of the transferable ruble and the national currencies could certainly smooth enterprise relations, and this effect has been suggested in recent Council Sessions. Such convertibility would, however, have a different meaning from that usually associated with currency convertibility.

There is little doubt that the present CMEA "reform agenda" envisages a new agreement on regional settlements, perhaps a European Payments Union-like arrangement suitably tailored to present CPE conditions and anchored to a reformed transferable ruble, and that regional price formation is likely to become more flexible in the near future, especially in the context of interenterprise relations (Haluska 1987; Leznik 1987; Rybalko 1988). A clear policy commitment on setting such prices in accordance with prevailing demand and supply rather than within extraneous parameters would signal a palpable change in socialist economic integration stances.

Currency convertibility could be critical in ensuring room for the smooth expansion of interenterprise contacts, in the concrete setting of effective prices, and in linking those prices with those of the domestic economies in accordance with prevailing price regulations. Given the disarray attending the ways in which scarcities are reflected in the policy instruments in place, however, a first step toward a more automatic kind of settlement of accounts should not be convertibility, even full regional convertibility of the transferable ruble. Instead, it might be feasible for CPE governments interested in bolstering direct contacts to negotiate about the expected volume of transactions of such interenterprise contacts. These ceilings could be revised, for example, on an annual basis. Within such agreed-upon quotas, settlements for all interenterprise transactions, first between any two CMEA countries and later among all interested members, perhaps through special accounts kept by the International Bank for Economic Cooperation, should be automatic and anonymous. Transactions exceeding the forecast volume may have to be dealt with initially within the regular settlements mechanism unless a supplementary agreement on incremental trade volumes can be hammered out. Imbalances that arise within the agreed global settlements volume, say at the end of each calendar year, could be cleared in different ways. I suggest it be done by the surplus country obtaining access to convertible currency loans from a common fund established by all interested countries, and increasingly by chronic deficit countries, that could be used only for expanding direct enterprise relations. Chronic deficit countries would have to pay in a rising proportion of their cumulative imbalance, on fulfillment of some conditions, in convertible currency. Remaining cumulative imbalances would have to be settled in an increasing proportion in convertible currency that could be appropriated only to foster interenterprise contacts.

There are clearly a number of similarities, as well as distinctions, between the above proposal and the European Payments Union's approach to convertibility. Recall that the latter took at least eight years—for Germany at least 11—to reach current account convertibility. The similarities are that the scheme calls for the automatic multilateral offsetting of bilateral surpluses and deficits incurred by each CMEA country vis-à-vis all other participants, although the offsetting would initially be confined to the products coming under direct enterprise relations. By extending these relations to a widening range of activities and a rapidly increasing volume of trade, their automatic nature would in time come to involve virtually all CMEA trade. Second, the proposal envisages partial settlement of imbalances in convertible currency that can be earmarked only to encourage interenterprise relations and hence to widen the scope of the scheme in a quasi-automatic fashion. Surplus countries would initially earn access to convertible currency loans intended to expand direct enterprise relations. Although there is some similarity in matching credits or fractional convertible currency settlements in the European Payments Union's approach (Triffin 1957, 163-94) and the one proposed here, the latter would be far more timid. A common fund of approximately 500 million in transferable rubles would be ample to start the scheme (Brabant 1989g). Whether the proposal should, as under the European Payments Union, impose settlements in convertible currency as the size of the imbalance exceeds quota is something that could be considered. If acceptable, it would certainly bolster the pressure from within to expand multilateral trade, but I fear that some CPEs may be reluctant to accept even the more modest version.

At the 43rd Council Session (October 12-14, 1987), Prime Minister Ryzhkov tabled a proposal for limited convertibility. Its limits would be threefold: (1) it would only affect CMEA transactions; (2) it would be introduced gradually over a period of ten years; and (3) it would apply initially only to selected goods, chiefly those coming within the compass of direct enterprise relations as provided for under the auspices of Scientific-technological Progress. This proposal was opposed by the German Democratic Republic, Romania, and Vietnam, but the other CMEA partners agreed to move ahead. In early 1988, the Soviet Union signed agreements with Bulgaria and Czechoslovakia with a view to implementing, beginning in 1989, the limited convertibility proposal in their bilateral relations. Bulgaria and Czechoslovakia also reached their bilateral agreement, which was to have gone into effect on September 1, 1988. Finally, the Soviet Union signed agreements with Mongolia.

In what respect does this proposal differ from either the European Payments Union or the one tabled here? Because I am not privy to the intramural debates and the proposal has not been laid out in detail, this question is difficult to answer. From interview material, it appears that the proposal envisages the automatic and anonymous clearing of selected transactions, but there is apparently no ceiling. Transactions would be conducted at local currency prices negotiated between partners on the basis of the Bucharest principles. The clearing of accounts would take place as for all other transferable ruble transactions, possibly after the local currency amounts were transformed into proper transferable ruble values by internal adjustment coefficients. Such coefficients would have been negotiated bilaterally in the meantime. Given the disarray in relative domestic prices and the difficulty of converting surpluses earned by individual firms, however, the scheme so far has not been very successful. It may die before receiving a fair trial.

The critical difference between the Ryzhkov proposal and the modest one outlined here is that the former does not have a prespecified volume within which clearing would be automatic and anonymous and imbalances would be subject to convertible currency "settlements" that can be earmarked only for the enhancement of direct enterprise relations. Without some such "stick" to enforce convertibility, I am afraid that the Ryzhkov proposal is likely to get bogged down very quickly by the serious problems of incompatible domestic prices and imbalances in the aggregate deliveries being offset by the regular trade accounting at the level of the International Bank for Economic Cooperation.

If the preceding is a correct reading of recent CMEA events and the momentous forthcoming session does not bring about a major change in the socialist economic integration mechanism, I am afraid that the so-called internal convertibility exercise will remain largely a nonstarter. I do not see how it could facilitate the settlements of obligations engaged in by decentralized producers and traders, except from a pure accounting perspective. Its potential to extend convertibility to all regional transactions and eventually to all trade is virtually nil; on the other hand, I believe the European Payments Union proposal and the more limited variant of it described here are potentially effective.

CONCLUSIONS

The observer of today's CMEA scene undoubtedly has reason for guarded optimism well beyond the expectations that could reasonably have been cherished, say, three years ago. Nonetheless, the proposal on enacting some kind of multilateralism and limited regional convertibility elaborated here may appear to be too timid. Likewise, my views on the realism of the convertibility debates in the CMEA in the past two years may be too skeptical, and hence my proposal may lag behind discussions made in the *sub rosa* CMEA. I am making these conservative proposals because I do not expect swift movement in the economic mechanism of socialist economic integration or in the pace of production integration to be achieved in the next few years. Second, I do not believe that all CMEA members are willing to rethink the regional economic integration mechanism from the ground up or to engage actively in interenterprise relations on anything but a trivial scale for years to come. Finally, the evidence for a reformed mechanism that has surfaced thus far has not been sufficiently reassuring for us to assume a major upswing in socialist economic integration is under way.

As the wave of market-minded reforms gains momentum in the CPEs that have already announced such intentions, and as it spreads geographically to include the key CMEA actors also in East Europe, a more positive step toward CMEA reform will become necessary. The CPEs that thus far have proved ready to introduce broad-based domestic reforms attuned to the regional economic mechanism should be in a position to progress faster and farther without being stymied by others, who voluntarily chose to postpone reforms. The socialist economic integration mechanism therefore should explicitly recognize that some members may remain in a transition phase different from others. An integration compact could be worked out in which the CPEs lay down an agreement on the degree to which each member can shield itself against "unfair competition" either from within or outside the CMEA. But such a functional degree of distinctiveness would be tolerated only if it did not undermine socialist economic integration from within or even prevent it altogether (see Brabant 1987d). The compact should also take issue with the pace at which the differences among the member countries are to be gradually eliminated and by what means.

REFERENCES

Allen, M. 1980. "Discussion." In *East European Integration and East-West Trade*. Eds. Paul Marer and John M. Montias. Bloomington, IN: Indiana University Press, pp. 142-44.

Altman, O. L. 1962. "L'or russe et le rouble." *Economie Appliquée* 3/4: 354-72.

Brabant, J. M. van. 1977. *East European Cooperation—The Role of Money and Finance*. New York: Praeger.

——. 1987a. *Adjustment, Structural Change, and Economic Efficiency—Aspects of Monetary Cooperation in Eastern Europe*. New York: Cambridge University Press.

——. 1987b. *Regional Price Formation in Eastern Europe—On the Theory and Practice of Trade Pricing*. Dordrecht: Kluwer Academic Publishers.

——. 1987c. "Economic Adjustment and the Future of Socialist Economic Integration." *Eastern European Politics and Society* 1: 75-112.

———. 1987d. "A Constitutional Framework for Economic Integration in Eastern Europe?" Paper presented at Columbia University, New York, April 27.

———. 1989a. *Economic Integration in Eastern Europe—A Handbook.* Hemel Hempstead: Harvester Wheatsheaf.

———. 1989b. "Socialist Countries and Development Assistance." In *Alternatives to Superpower Competition in the Third World: Latin America and Beyond.* Ed. John F. Weeks. New York: New York University Press. Forthcoming.

———. 1989c. "Regional Integration, Economic Reforms, and Convertibility." *Jahrbuch der Wirtschaft Osteuropas (Yearbook of East European Economics)* 13: 1. Forthcoming.

———. 1989d. "Integration Reform: New Horizons for the CMEA and East-West Economic Relations?" In *Perestroika and East-West Economic Relations: Prospects for the 1990s.* Eds. Michael Kraus and Ronald D. Liebowitz. New York: New York University Press.

———. 1989e. "The Role of Governments in Planned Economies—A Discussion." In *The Impact of Governments on East-West Economic Relations.* Eds. Gary Bertsch and Christopher Saunders. London: Macmillan (for the Wiener Institut fur Internationale Wirtschaftsvergleiche). Forthcoming.

———. 1989f. "Economic Reforms and Convertibility in Eastern Europe." In *Le economie socialiste.* Eds. Claudio de Vincenti and M. Mulino. Naples: Ligouri. Forthcoming.

———. 1989g. "Economic Reform and Monetary Cooperation in the CMEA." In *Financial Reform in Socialist Economies.* Eds. Christine Kessides, Timothy King, Mario Nuti, and Catherine Sokil. Washington, DC: World Bank, pp. 170-95.

———. 1989h. "Socialist Economics and Disequilibrium—Kornai versus Portes." *Journal of Economic Perspectives* 2. Forthcoming.

———. 1990a. *Centrally Planned Economies and International Economic Organizations.* Cambridge: Cambridge Univiversity. Forthcoming.

———. 1990b. "Wither the CMEA?—Reconstructing Socialist Economic Integration." *Osteuropa-Wirtschaft* 2. Forthcoming.

Colombatto, E. 1983. "CMEA, Money and Ruble Convertibility." *Applied Economics* 4: 479-506.

Dubrowsky, H. J. 1989. "Aspekte der Konvertierbarkeit sozialistischer Währungen." *Wirtschaftswissenschaft* 5: 712-34.

Dunajewski, H. 1979. "Quelques observations sur la fonction internationale des monnaies des pays de l'Europe de l'Est." *Revue d'Etudes Comparatives Est-Ouest* 4: 195-204.

Edwards, R. W., Jr. 1985. *International Monetary Collaboration.* Dobbs Ferry, NY: Transnational Publishers.

Fedorowicz, Z. 1975. *Podstawy teorii pienidza w gospodarce socialistycznej.* Warsaw: PWE.

———. 1979. "La convertibilité du rouble transférable." *Revue d'Etudes Comparatives Est-Ouest* 4: 177-83.

Gold, J. 1971. "The Fund's Concept of Convertibility." IMF Pamphlet Series, No. 14.

Grinev, V. S. 1987. "Perestrojka vnesneekonomiceskogo kompleksa." *Vnesnjaja torgovlju* 5: 2-5.

Haluska, I. 1987. "Pôsobenie cien na rozvoj priamych vzt'ahov v rámci RVHP." *Finance a úver* 5: 289-92.

Horcicová, M. 1987. "Proc nebyly splneny cíle komplexního programu z roku 1971? Smenitelnost: nutnost, nikoliv prání." *Hospodárské Noviny* 28: 5.

———. 1989. "Smenitelnost cs. koruny: prostredek, cil a vysledek." *Finance a úver* 5: 289-97.

IMF. 1978. *Articles of Agreement.* Washington, DC: International Monetary Fund.

———. 1988. *Yearbook of Foreign Exchange Restrictions.* Washington, DC: International Monetary Fund.

Kazandzieva, Kina. 1983. "Konvertiruemost na socialisticeskite valuti pri suvremenite uslovija." *Finansi i kredit* 8: 27-37.

Konstantinov, J. A. 1983. "Vzaimodejstvie na nacionalnite valuti s mezdunarodnata socialisticeska valuta." *Finansi i kredit* 2: 3-15.

———. 1987. "Prjamye svjazi v ramkach SEV: ich valjutno-finansovoe obespecenie." *Finansy SSSR* 4: 54-60.

Krzak, M. K. 1987. "W kierunku wymienalnosci rubla transferowego." *Zycie Gospodarcze* 9: 1,4.

Leznik, A. 1987. "Upravlenie mezdunarodnoj naucno-proizvod-stvennoj kooperaciej stran SEV." *Planovoe chozjajstvo* 4: 23-30.

Nuti, D. M. 1989. "Feasible Financial Innovation Under Market Socialism." In *Financial Reform in Socialist Economies.* Eds. Christine Kessides, Timothy King, Mario Nuti, and Catherine Sokil. Washington, DC: The World Bank, pp. 85-105.

Ondrácek, M. 1983. "Pristupy ekonomu socialistickych zemí k resení menové problematiky RVHP—úloha menovych kursu (koeficientu) v plánovite rizené ekonomice." *Finance a úver* 1: 60-69.

Petrakov, N. J. 1987. "Planovaja cena v sisteme upravlenija narodnym chozjajstvom." *Voprosy ekonomiki* 1: 44-55.

Rybalko, G. 1987. "Aktivnaya rol' valjutnogo mechanizma." *Ekonomiceskaja gazeta* 11: 20.

———. 1987. "Konvertabel'nost' rublya v povestke dnja." *Ekonomiceskaja gazeta* 11: 20.

Tokareva, P. A., M. D. Kudrjasov, and V. I. Morozov, eds. 1972. *Mnogostoronnee ekonomiceskoe sotrudnicestvo socialisticeskich gosudarstv—sbornik dokumentov.* Moscow: Juridiceskaya literatura.

Triffin, R. 1957. *Europe and the Money Muddle—From Bilateralism to Near-Convertibility, 1947-1956.* New Haven and London: Yale University Press.

Wiles, P. J. 1973. "On Purely Financial Convertibility." In *Banking, Money and Credit in Eastern Europe.* Ed. Yves Laulan. Brussels: NATO Directorate, pp. 119-25.

Válek, V. 1985. "Zdokonalování devizove financního mechanismu v rámci RVHP." *Zahranicní Obchod* 8, 10-14.

———. 1987. "Uloha tvorby cen a devizového zúctování pri rozvoji vyssích forem spoluprárce v rámci RVHP." *Zahranicní Obchod* 4: 12-16.

Vostavek, J. 1987. "Smenitelnost zrcadlim ekonomiky." *Hospodárské Noviny* 17: 3.

CHAPTER 7

The Hungarian Approach to Convertibility

KALMAN MIZSEI

In 1975, a leading Hungarian economist concluded his article on economic reform in the following way: "I think it is justified to approach convertibility gradually. Our backwardness in this field is doubtless. Lack of recognition of this is no less a danger than a decision to take measures surpassing our development and capacities. An even bigger mistake would be, however, to see the key to faster economic growth in convertibility. On the road to progressive convertibility the first steps . . . should not be rash measures in the expectations of miraculous results" (Kopatsy 1975). Fourteen years later, a Hungarian expert on foreign economic relations commented, "Nowadays there are many who condemn the tactics of small steps, and with full right: the small steps usually end in retreat and degenerate into standing in one place. Still, I believe that jumping in one place does not lead forward either, and the declaration of external convertibility prematurely would be something like that" (Szegvari 1989). Both authors caution against the all-too-common approach of many economic politicians and sometimes even scholars to convertibility. Because the word "convertibility" can be defined in various ways, I will use it in a limited sense, as it is understood in postwar West Europe, for the sake of brevity.

What is the origin of demands for declaration of convertibility before the development of a mature market economy in East

Europe? One is relatively simple: convertibility sounds nice; as an economic policy goal, it is very saleable abroad. Even the international financial institutions, especially the International Monetary Fund (IMF), usually press for it. But the desire has other origins, the sources of which come from inside rather than outside the country. If economic policymakers and officials ignore the objective tools of measurement in macroeconomic and microeconomic decisionmaking, they will suffer the consequences. What is the price one has to pay for hard currency imports in terms of domestic currency? Is a given export profitable? How efficient is trade with other members of the CMEA? These are questions one cannot answer without introducing a convertible currency.

In this argument, however, the real relationships are turned upside down. The core of the problem is the Soviet-type socialist economic system that tried to ban market integration of the society and deliberately isolated the domestic economy from the world market. Convertibility, therefore, will probably be the result of a long-lasting process of market reform in the economic system, including the sphere of foreign economic relations, and not an instrument of the current reform process or, as is sometimes silently hoped, the instrument helping to avert the pains of market reform.

I. THE HUNGARIAN REFORM OF 1968 AND EXTERNAL RELATIONS

The reform concept before 1968 mirrored in a very odd way the ideology of the earlier socialist period because its authors were thinking in the categories of an autarkic, closed economy. Therefore, the new economic mechanism (NEM) did not have an elaborate program to change the way in which Hungary's foreign economic affairs were managed. This does not mean that a subcommission was not established to consider trade reforms, but rather that foreign trade did not fit organically into mainstream reform proposals. The economists of that time implicitly supposed that the reform would increase the general efficiency of the economy to such an extent that "the one who has forints can have foreign currency as well" principle would apply. With the terminology of János Kornai, the assumption that the reform would create hard budget constraints was implicit in the reform concept (Mizsei

1987a; Rosati and Mizsei 1989). The domestic economic reform did not, however, establish such conditions, as is apparent from the extensive literature listing the failures of the NEM and explaining the reasons for these failures.

Until the mid-1980s, ideologically cautious critiques of the reform sought to demonstrate that the problem had been deformations in the course of realization rather than in the concept behind the NEM. Only recently has it been recognized that the very concept of market simulation instead of genuine market regulation was the primary reason for the shortcomings of the Hungarian reform (Mizsei 1988). In other words, the Hungarian reform tried to imitate the enterprises and the macroeconomic policy environment of the western market economies without reproducing the basic incentive structure inherent to them, that is, the ownership structure.[1]

In spite of this, Hungary's foreign economic relations developed quickly, and equilibrium was maintained during the first few years of the reform. One of the reasons was external: until 1973, the world economy expanded rapidly, prices were remarkably stable, and it was the period of the first East-West détente. The environment was favorable for a centrally managed economy with limited, but expanding, autonomy of enterprises. At the same time, the lack of major price restructuring processes made it easy for economic policymakers to distribute scarce foreign resources on the basis of an implicit ratchet principle. Steady export expansion made it possible for imports to grow every year as well. In this relatively stable and foreseeable environment, the limited decentralization of decisionmaking under NEM brought about more positive than adverse effects.

Export expansion in this period was by no means the result of a well-designed and comprehensive export-oriented strategy; it was, rather, a result the enterprises' need for scarce import goods and the favorable external conditions. Economic policy at that time

---

1. When Kornai speaks about hard and soft budget constraints, he means that the lack of the possibility of bankruptcy in the reformed economy prevents the system from exercising necessary financial discipline on economic agents. Similarly, the lack of free entrance of new firms stabilizes the position of monopolies to the extent that the Hungary of that period was qualitatively different from a true market economy.

concentrated on expanding trade and cooperation with the Soviet Union, in such a way that the Soviets provided the necessary raw material and energy resources for economic growth, while Soviet demand for rather low-quality Hungarian export goods, primarily manufactured industrial products and machinery, was practically inexhaustible. From the point of view of the reform, and especially of convertibility, this was a harmful policy, because such a pattern of trade influenced very adversely the Hungarian economic system. In contrast, expanding western trade connections—with their more demanding quality requirements, standards, and business practices—would have had a positive impact on the economic system.

The 1968 reform initiated a process of loosening of the institutional rigidity of foreign trade, but this process did not proceed very far at that time because of a very early change in the reform policy (Wass von Czege 1980). Generally, institutional openness was not achieved in this first reform wave; the foreign trade monopoly, meaning the bureaucratic monopoly of the foreign trade enterprises, was not changed. Foreign trade enterprises maintained excessive power to determine the validity of the import requirements of the producers, while the rights of foreign trade enterprises to use their earnings from foreign trade activity were much more limited than those of industrial firms (Gacs 1980).

The common understanding of the dynamics of the Hungarian reform is that its expansive period lasted from 1968-1972, and a more conservative course prevailed from then until the end of the 1970s. This picture is roughly correct as far as the macropolitical course is concerned. From our point of view, however, this problem is usually neglected in the scholarly thinking about convertibility. Therefore, the question I wish to address here is the so-called internal convertibility of the domestic currency. This notion is misleading, because it is used two different ways in the literature. Here we use it in the sense of the freedom of economic actors to use their domestic currency for different purposes.

In this sense, the 1968 reform was extremely cautious; transfer of money between the different enterprise funds—for example, funds for investment and wages—was very difficult, and a loosening up of this system followed rather gradually, not in keeping with the cyclical character of political struggles over reform. From 1968-

1975, how to divide the profit of the enterprise among investment, bonus, and reserve funds was centrally determined. It is true that the firms always found some way to avoid the rules and to channel money from "softer" to "harder" funds. Generally, the wage and bonus funds are the "hardest," but firms circumvent limits on wage and bonus payments by contracting with private firms and workers' organizations, thus converting labor costs from the category of wages to that of costs of production, which are less subject to control.

A qualitative change in this respect came in 1976. Central control over fund distribution was replaced by a system of secondary taxation. Enterprises divided their profits freely among funds, but an overly rapid growth of wages or bonuses, and sometimes also of the development fund for investments, was a target of prohibitive secondary taxes, which were imposed in addition to the normal profits tax. This system left more freedom for the firms, but, compared to a classical market environment, it still hampered the expansion of profitable activities. Economic policy alone, however, could not eliminate these barriers because of the property problem. The enterprises would increase the wages of employees and expand firms beyond their real opportunities because they had no hard budget constraint and the threat of bankruptcy was nonexistent. The dominance of state-owned property rendered the problem impossible to solve.

Enterprises have naturally exerted pressure to lift the barriers that have created many absurdities in the day-to-day life of the management. In 1989, the separate wage regulation was abolished, which inevitably caused enormous inflationary pressures. I will return to this question later in the context of the recent economic policy.

The structural changes in the world economy after 1973 have affected the problem of currency convertibility. The Hungarian economic system's adjustment to major restructuring in international price relations was, as one could logically expect, quite poor. Inflation was still approached in an ideological way. Socialism was considered to be free of inflation, and the central authorities thus tried to neutralize the impact of the international price increases on the domestic firms so that they were not obliged to transfer this impact to consumer markets. The other harmful aspect of the ideological approach was that politicians tried to con-

vince themselves of and to propagate the idea that socialist international economic cooperation prevents capitalist inflation from influencing our prices. In reality, this could be achieved only by a
sharp increase in subsidies to the enterprises and to consumer
prices.

Such subsidies wreaked havoc on the budget and the entire foreign trade system in the late 1970s because increased budget expenditures had to be compensated by centralization of resources
from elsewhere. Furthermore, it had a very demoralizing impact
on the domestic enterprises because costs became unimportant. The
budget subsidized low-efficiency production and exports and
imports, while reducing the revenues of units with higher efficiency. In this ideological environment, exchange rate policy had
to serve the short-term anti-inflationary goals by overvaluing the
domestic currency, which further increased the budget redistribution. The commercial exchange rate was, in principle, unified, but
in practice the budget interference weakened the importance of it
or, in other words, established different effective exchange rates for
different transactions.

I mentioned earlier that the dynamic expansion of Hungary's
trade with the hard currency area made the relationship of the
macroeconomic organs with the enterprises relatively smooth in
the first half of the 1970s. After the oil shock, economic policymakers had to decide whether to put stricter conditions on the enterprises and decrease the volume of available hard currency resources or to follow the old path of expanding western imports,
which now had to mean increasingly negative trade balances. In
the given political framework, the short-run interests of the apparatus prevailed: indebtedness was a more painless option.

II. INDEBTEDNESS AND THE PROSPECTS FOR CONVERTIBILITY

By the end of the 1970s, indebtedness had fundamentally changed
the conditions for systemic reform and, as a part of it, for convertibility. The effects of the growing external debt were many and
contradictory. Beginning approximately in 1979, the leadership
gave way to renewed public debates on reform in the face of a potential political crisis. As a result of these debates and the spontaneous

economic policy actions undertaken, many changes were introduced in the institutional framework, as well as in macroeconomic regulation. Because these measures are well known, I will mention them only briefly. Efforts were made to deconcentrate the organizational structure of the economy. Branch ministries were amalgamated, and large, monopolistic enterprises were split up into smaller units. This campaign did not, however, produce spectacular results. The formation of small, quasi-private units was made easier (Antal 1985).

To overcome the above-mentioned isolation of the Hungarian price structure and economic environment from the world market, a poorly designed price reform was introduced in 1980. The purpose of the reform was to imitate the world market price of commodities on the domestic market through an inevitably complicated set of rules. The idea of the then-chairman of the Price Office was that convertibility would be a realistic target after full implementation of the new price rules. This idea fit into the general market simulation strategy of the Hungarian reforms in the sense that the economic reformers wanted to simulate market signals instead of relying on free prices. The price rules naturally could not be implemented fully, but even so, they caused great harm in many ways, and the prospects for convertibility became even more remote than before.

In addition, the question of convertibility became topical because Hungary, under the pressure of its external debt, finally gathered the necessary political courage and applied for membership to the IMF and the World Bank in 1981. Membership undoubtedly helped to overcome the debt crisis of 1982, which broke out as a result of the political developments in Poland, but it also raised the convertibility question in a fundamental way. The IMF and the World Bank tried to apply economic policy measures to Hungary as if it were a market economy. They urged policy steps toward convertibility without demanding fundamental reforms in the ownership structure. This misunderstanding also contributed to the confusion about the real preconditions for convertibility.

Two contradictory foreign trade regulation trends prevailed in the first half of the 1980s. The monopoly of the trade enterprises of imports and exports was gradually loosened as producing enterprises were given greater rights to direct participation in foreign trade. The objective of this organizational change was to increase the interest of the firms in exports. Therefore, it was easier to get licenses to export than to import. The country's import regime became very bureaucratic in 1982 in the wake of the critical external payment situation. The administration did not opt for decreasing import demand or increasing export incentives by an active exchange rate policy because of concerns about inflation, and also because they were not confident that enterprises would respond to price changes (and they were right). What remained was administrative import control, especially the strengthening of the central distribution of import quotas. There was no way to avoid such reliance on direct controls in the existing system conditions. However, this administrative import regime lasted too long, because a concentrated reform policy, including property reform as a major component, was not implemented at the same time. Administrative methods in foreign trade generated similar central interference in other fields as well.

Under pressure from the IMF, Hungary adopted an active exchange rate policy in 1982, calling for effective devaluation of the forint. However, this intention was not put into practice, and Hungarian exchange rate devaluations reflected only inflation. Thus, effectively, no devaluation took place until 1985 (Oblath 1987). This approach to exchange rate policy has not changed in recent years, and short-term concern about inflation still has priority.

Restrictive macroeconomic policies increased the political tensions between the center and the enterprises, as well as between the center and the population. To ease these tensions, the government opted for an acceleration policy in 1985. This aggravated the balance-of-payments problem almost immediately, and the economic policy cycle resumed. In the last two years, however, some important new phenomena have occurred that bear on the convertibility of the forint.

It was obvious that the operations of the 1982-1984 period were hardly repeatable, because the economy was in worse shape due to the continuous trade restrictions, and new methods had to be found. At the same time, changes on the political level opened the way for new initiatives, especially after the nomination of Grosz for Prime Minister in 1987. The new reform wave was represented by a tax reform, which should be included among the market simulation measures, new incentives for private enterprise, liberalized joint-venture legislation, formation of a two-tier banking system, and a commitment to a tough monetary policy.

The problem of money supply requires further discussion. In the pre-1988 period, separate regulation of the different markets—consumer and investment, for example—by means of the above-mentioned system of secondary taxation attempted to secure market equilibrium. By means of financial deregulation, the abolition of this complicated system of secondary taxes should have been replaced by a unified monetary policy. This effort thus aimed to contribute to making the domestic currency internally convertible (as the concept has been used in this paper). This kind of economic policy is unique in the economic history of socialist Hungary, and it has provided us with very interesting insights on the applicability of such policy in a situation characterized by the dominance of state property.

First of all, one should notice that the case of tax reform in 1988 was entangled with the efforts of the financial authorities to increase state revenues. Therefore, the value-added tax was fixed at the very high level of 25 percent. The inflation in that year, for this technical reason, had to be higher than in the earlier period. However, authorities tried to avoid major inflation beyond the purely technical consequences of the new tax system. Also, because of these financial changes and to avoid a wage-price spiral, the 1988 wage regulation was very rigid, and it also tried to contribute to a significant cut in real wages. Authorities made sure that the centralized wage regulation was only transitional and that a complete abolition of separate wage regulation would follow in 1989. As it turns out, wage increases in 1988 were significantly below the price inflation, but in the circumstances of a liberalized policy, employees' incomes grew very fast in the following year. In the field of wage policy, 1989 is the real test case because 1988 was atypical.

The other crucial objective of monetary policy is enterprise behavior. Sharp limits on the money supply make the profit prospects of enterprises bleaker. In a market environment, a weeding-out of inefficient firms would follow according to market efficiency. In the Hungarian case, however, the financial discipline of the enterprises has not improved due to a lack of the threat of bankruptcy. There surely is bankruptcy legislation in Hungary, but it is unreliable; because there are no real owners of assets, it is not easy to find real losers. Furthermore, the political center is too weak to force through costly and politically divisive bankruptcy procedures. The absence of freely determined market prices also makes it hard to justify the case for bankruptcy.

In this situation, enterprises can easily postpone payments to each other and to banks. In circumstances of inflation, it is even profitable because it effectively creates loans with interest payments. Unrealized payments have accumulated in the period of tough monetary policy, putting the financial system under an enormous strain. In this situation, the financial authorities must increase the money supply, otherwise relations among firms will be impaired. In addition, this situation—with harder budget constraints—hurts private firms more. Consequently, inflation will inevitably increase. This does not mean that tough monetary policy is useless, it simply means that monetary policy must be linked with a radical privatization scheme so that the average hardness of the budget constraint grows. Bankruptcy should be a part of the privatization measures because the property structure of the sold bankrupt firms would most likely be more private than previously if no restrictions on privatization existed.

The monetary policy of the last 18 months has brought some successes as well (Mizsei and Torok 1989). Market competition has increased in several commodity groups as a consequence of the scarcity of money among firms and households. The inflationary pressure caused by the liberal wage policy is less than in the case of the other reform economies in East Europe, in part due to this monetary policy and in part due to the personal income tax, which moderates the net effect of the gross wage increase.

Another important positive effect of monetary policy is that it aided the liberalization of a share of hard currency imports in 1989. Before discussing this measure, we must turn our attention first to the developments in the field of import regulation in 1988. The problem of administrative import restrictions was so important that economic policymakers were pressed to initiate new solutions. The so-called saldo regulation was a very modest relative of the internationally known retention quota system. Participation in this system was voluntary and was based on a certain degree of improvement in the balance of foreign trade in hard currencies of the enterprise. The benefit from it was that firms had greater freedom in their import decisions as well as in the timing of the purchases. Furthermore, a certain amount of the additional improvement in the balance could increase the import quota of the enterprise automatically. The degree of participation of the companies was high because they had extensive untapped opportunities for improved performance in their foreign trade. The saldo regulation proved to be a strong export incentive in 1988.

This system could have been extended in 1989, or a full retention quota system could have been introduced, as many scholars urged (Mizsei 1987; Szegvari 1989). The argument for the retention quota system is that it permits a gradualist approach, it has strong export incentives, and, most notably, its gradual expansion can lead to convertibility of the domestic currency. According to the advocates of this system, it necessarily should be complemented with the institution of a hard currency exchange so that exchanges of hard currency holdings among enterprises could be promoted. It is also important that bargaining between the center and the enterprises about the level of the quotas should be discouraged by establishing as clear rules for setting the level of quotas as possible. I proposed fully unified quotas starting at a rather high level, about 50 percent, because otherwise the positive effect of the retention scheme would be minor, and the likelihood of retreat would be very high. Other authors have proposed a system that would consider the level of value added in fixing the quotas: the more sophisticated the goods, the higher the quotas (Szegvari 1989).

Introduction of retention quotas and a hard currency exchange undoubtedly would have an inflationary effect because the import demand of the enterprises is such that they are eager to pay a great deal for the opportunity to buy goods in the market economies. The other objection to the system is that it has an adverse impact on the domestic cooperation among enterprises because everybody wants to export (Salgo 1988). Therefore, and because of IMF requirements, the Hungarian authorities opted for import liberalization according to commodity lists, as suggested by some experts (Gacs 1987). In 1989, approximately one-quarter of the imports were liberalized. As I mentioned, it did not lead to an import growth at an unmanageable level in the first half of 1989 due to the restrictive monetary policy and some technical measures that made imports more ex-

pensive. However, if I am correct that the recent tough monetary
policy is unsustainable for much longer, it also means that relaxation of the money supply will have an immediate effect on the
import demand of the firms. This could then jeopardize the import rules as well. Recent plans to extend the ratio of liberalized
goods to 40 percent in the next year seem to be overly optimistic.
Whether one or the other sort of gradual import liberalization
will be more feasible, one thing is certain: a precondition for the
success of import liberalization is a simultaneous and radical shift
of the ownership structure in the economy toward private property
so that a tough monetary policy can be applied.

For more than a decade, the major source of macroeconomic loss
in Hungary has been the obsolete and highly inefficient cooperation pattern among the socialist states (Inotai 1986). Most of the
suggested solutions here have shortcomings similar to those of the
approaches to convertibility. The authors of reform proposals tend
to neglect the fact that the cooperation pattern is a logical consequence of the domestic environment. Therefore, the declaration of
willingness of the politicians to switch intra-CMEA trade to a dollar base, as was proposed recently in Hungary, will not solve the
problems. Arguments on behalf of the gradualist approach to dollarization include: it would mean a return to the old pattern; it
would give a clear picture which part of the trade is efficient and
weed out the rest; it would free us from the harms of barter trade; it
would contribute consequently to the necessary cuts in the mutual
trade of soft commodities; and, finally, it would increase Hungary's
attractiveness to foreign investors because they could have access to
the huge Soviet market.

Without a firm foundation in the reform process in general,
this kind of transformation would most likely have a negative effect. Because of the commodity structure of intra-CMEA trade,
Hungary would most likely suffer in short run because the commodity composition of this trade cannot be changed fundamentally, and there is no reason to suppose that short-run losses would
be manageable for Hungary. Furthermore, the big Hungarian
manufacturing exporters on the Soviet market could efficiently exert pressure on Hungarian authorities to soften the rules and give
them barter contingents according to recent precedents. The recent construction of a complicated barter trade is based on a tradi-

tion that is important in the case of rigid partners, as the Hungarian and especially the Soviet trading authorities are. If the proposed radical shift would be implemented, the Soviet authorities would stop buying commodities that they usually do not buy for hard currencies. The most likely outcome of such an unrealistic jump would be a quick return to the well-known practice where the partners would be especially keen to avoid imbalances in bilateral trade because both are short of hard currency.

A more adequate approach would be the one that takes the recent stage of development of the domestic economic systems into account. It could leave the more sensitive part of barter trade almost unchanged, and for the rest it could declare decentralized decision-making and the use of domestic currencies with the full responsibility of the exporters to find import demand among the domestic firms for the given amount of foreign currency. The forint-transferable ruble exchange rate should be floated. The scope of this part of the trade should be extended gradually in the following years (Szegvari 1989).

Economic reform of the kind that would lead to convertibility of the national currency needs a strong government and an especially well-coordinated set of measures. The professional skills for such a reform package might exist in Hungary, but it is unclear whether the country will be able to formulate and implement strong macroeconomic policies in the foreseeable future. The new government that will emerge from the democratic elections to be held in the spring of 1990 might have the necessary legitimacy to start with tough, sometimes unpopular, decisions. It is also possible that the recent erosion, rather than reform, of the economic system will continue. Some degree of "Polandization" of the Hungarian economy is not an insignificant danger. In this case, its displacement by a convertible currency—such as the dollar in the Polish case and the deutsche mark in the Yugoslav case—not convertibility of the domestic currency, would follow. The role of foreign currencies has already increased in the last couple of years in Hungary, but the chances for avoiding dollarization exist. The exchange rate is much lower than in the two above-mentioned countries, and the privatization process will probably start on a full scale when the domestic economy is not as disorganized and inflation is not as damaging as in Yugoslavia or Poland (Topinski

1989). The sequence and space of decentralization will be extremely important in this case.

REFERENCES

Antal, L. 1985. *Gazdasagiranyitasi Rendszerunk A Reform Utjan.* Budapest: KJK.
Gacs, J. 1980. Importkorlatok, Hianyjelensegek es a Vallalati Alkalmazkodas. Budapest.
Kopatsy, S. 1975. "A Konvertibilitasrol." *Kozgazdasagi Szemle,* No. 11.
Mizsei, K. 1987a. "A Comparative Analysis of Hungarian and Polish Economic Reform Theories." *Jahrbuch der Wirtschaft Osteuropas* 12, 1.
——. 1987b. A Valutavisszateritesi Rendszer a Gazdasag Intezmenyi Nyitottsaganak Eszkoze. *Tervgazdasagi Forum,* No. 1.
——. 1988. "Is the Hungarian Economic Mechanism a Model to be Emulated?" *Eastern European Economics* 2, 4.
Mizsei, K., and A. Torok. 1989. "Modified Planned Economies at the Crossroads: The Case of Hungary." Forthcoming manuscript. Helsinki: WIDER.
Oblath, G. 1987. *Az Arfolyampolitika Helye a Reformcsomagban.* Budapest: KOPINT.
Rosati, D., and K. Mizsei. 1989. "Adjustment through Opening of Socialist Economies." WIDER Working Papers, World Institute for Development Economics Research of the United Nations University, Helsinki, January.
Salgo, I. 1988. "Az Importliberalizacio Alternativai." *Kulgazdasag,* No. 11.
Szegvari, I. 1989. "Forintkonvertibilitas es a Realitasok." *Figyelo,* No. 20.
Topinski, A. 1989. "A Piaci Egyensulyhiany Okai." *Tervgazdasagi Forum,* No. 4. Forthcoming.
Wass von Czege, A. 1980. *Ungarns Aussenwirtschaftsmodell Eine Untersuchung des Spannungsfeldes Zwischen OstWest Kooperation und RGW Integration.* Oekonomische Studien No. 28, University of Hamburg.

Joint Ventures in Poland

CHAPTER 8

Joint Ventures with Foreign Capital in Poland: From Ideology to Market System

KRZYSZTOF A. LIS *and* HENRYK STERNICZUK

I. INTRODUCTION

In this paper we examine the development of regulations for the establishment and operation of foreign investments and joint ventures between western firms and individuals and Polish enterprises. We will see what vast changes communist states have made in the organization of productive activity, evolving from autarky in the 1950s to joint ventures and foreign-owned enterprises in the 1980s. To show what kinds of economic events we are discussing and their magnitude, we begin with some statistics describing the latest developments in the formation of joint ventures.

Joint ventures between western investors and Polish enterprises are a relatively new phenomenon in the Polish economy. Certain forms of a foreign presence in the economy were allowed beginning in 1976,[1] but specific regulations regarding joint ventures were issued by the Polish Parliament only in 1986. We refer here to the Law on Companies with Foreign Capital Participation of April 12, 1986.[2] According to the Polish Chamber of Foreign Trade, in 1987-1988, about 200 Polish state enterprises sought opportunities to engage in a joint venture with a foreign partner (Lis

1. *Monitor Polski,* No. 15, Item 110.
2. *Dziennik Ustaw,* No. 17, Item 88.

1987). At the same time, almost 100 negotiations were conducted, although only 20 of them ended with registration of a new company by the end of 1987. Since then, a new law established with an effective date of January 1, 1989, has changed the legal and political framework for foreign capital participation in the Polish economy. According to H. Janiszewski, Vice-Chairman of the Agency for Foreign Investment, by August 27, 1989, 250 joint ventures with western capital were registered in Poland (Janiszewski 1989). The Agency estimates that by the end of 1989 there will be approximately 500 joint ventures. In fact, the number of new organizations increases very fast. Four months after the introduction of the new law of 1989, four times as many joint ventures were formed as in the period 1986-1988. Statistical data available to us cover 203 joint ventures, that is, 81.2 percent of all registered joint ventures (Janiszewski 1989). Their capital stock is 41 billion zloty, which equals about US$5.1 million at the black market exchange rate and US$51 million at the official exchange rate. Of this total capital, foreign investment makes up US$220 million, which is 176 billion zloty at the official exchange rate. The largest group of joint ventures, 32 percent of the total, operates in the food processing industry. The tourist service industry accounts for 20.68 percent of all ventures; the construction industry, 16.25 percent; the electronic industry, 11.33 percent; the chemical industry, 9.85 percent; the environmental protection industry, 2.46 percent; and 7.38 percent is connected with all other industries of the Polish economy. About one-third of all joint ventures have their headquarters in Warsaw.

What do these numbers mean? All we can say now is that we observe a good beginning of involvement of the Polish economy in the international division of labor. These processes were frozen by Communist Party policy and legislation for 40 years, and thus the slow development of progress in this area is understandable. Despite that, the growth of joint ventures is quite significant when we take the chaotic condition of the Polish economy into account. That 250 joint ventures with foreign capital formed in three years that the economy has been in deep crisis is a significant achievement. However, the transition from domestic state to privately owned companies was much more dynamic at the time. In 1988, 26,744 private joint stock companies were formed in Poland, and

17,738 were established during 1986-1988 (Iwanowska and Sterniczuk 1989). A comparison in terms of financial investment looks much better because foreign investors invested in 203 joint stock companies that also had Polish investors, a total of US$220 million, while 840 fully owned small businesses have capital of US$120 million.

II. HISTORICAL BACKGROUND ON RULES FOR WESTERN CAPITAL INVESTMENT IN THE POLISH ECONOMY

Despite the significant reforms undertaken recently, communist states are still far from the point where their economic systems are governed entirely by the market, but they are also very far from the point where they were before Stalin's death. Soviet communism used to have a rigid, hard-line approach to the existence of capitalist institutions and mechanisms in the economy. However, the economic crisis in the Soviet Union in the 1920s was overcome thanks to capitalist organizational forms introduced as part of Lenin's New Economic Policy (NEP). Among these was foreign direct investment in the Soviet Union by western firms. As economists pointed out, "NEP assumed only the temporary access of capitalist elements to the communist economy. The Communist Party maintained control over the signals emanating from the capitalist market and set up rules for a reduction of capitalist forms in the communist economy" (Brus and Pohorille 1953a, 83). From the beginning, NEP was accepted only as a tactic for overcoming internal economic problems, such as hunger, and the extremely low productivity of newly socialized enterprises. NEP was cancelled as soon as the economic situation improved because the party's objective was a continuation of the communist order and not the formation of an affluent society.

The situation was much clearer under Stalin. Market economy organization was one-dimensionally identified with the exploitation and pauperization of the working class. The export of capital was, in communist ideology and policy, the worst strategy, leading to the deepest damage to the economic systems of other countries. According to Nikolai Bukharin (1934, 130), "The export of capital is the most convenient means for financial groups to gain control over new areas." Another Communist Party official, G. Malenkow (1952, 22), 20 years later expressed the same opinion.

Obviously, the opinions of Soviet leaders affected the economic policy of the new communist countries established after World War II under Soviet supervision. Before 1939, Polish industries had mixed domestic and foreign ownership. For example, in the mining and steel industries, 52.5 percent of the capital belonged to foreign investors; in the oil industry, 87.5 percent; in the electric industry, 66.1 percent; and in the chemical industry, 59.9 percent (Minc 1946, 14, 15).

Immediately after the war, the economic policy of the new Polish government did not exclude economic collaboration with western countries. The policy conducted in that period reflected a coalition type of government including both the Social Democratic and Communist parties. C.Z. Bobrowski, Chairman of the Central Planning Office, a leading agency for economic policy design, expressed the socialist position in this way: ". . . foreign loans are important conditions for the realization of our plans. We cannot think about the achievement of our goals without the participation of foreign capital. There is no reason not to assume that a process of slow but constant inflow of foreign capital will continue" (Bobrowski 1946, 42). At that time, even the communist faction assumed that about 20 percent of the capital necessary for investment plans would come from western loans (Minc 1946, 28). This moderate policy of the coalition government turned around dramatically in 1948 after the liquidation of the Central Planning Office, the unification of all political parties, and the further strengthening of the communist order in Poland. In the next period of hardline communist policy, only limited trade between western and eastern countries was permitted, while other forms of international economic relations were condemned.

After Stalin's death, policy relaxation again made international collaboration an object of public debate. Hard currency shortages became among the most difficult obstacles to economic development. Despite that, direct investment of foreign capital in the Polish economy was still not accepted due to the dogma of communism, which maintained its sway throughout the 1950s and 1960s. To cope with shortages of many products and with technical stagnation, Polish and other East European regimes chose to buy licenses rather than to give foreign companies access to the domestic market. In the 1960s, and with higher intensity in the 1970s, there was extensive purchasing of patents, licenses, machines, and whole technological lines for manufacturing. Purchases were financed through large loans from western countries. While architects of this policy believed that they would be able to pay back these loans through the export of goods and services from modernized industries, it did not occur. These investments never paid off to the extent expected. Thus, this strategy was an expensive solution that never completely succeeded in fully modernizing the economy. Causes of the failure were deeply rooted in the politically, rather than economically, driven mechanisms for the allocation of capital in the communist system, in the lack of market orientation of enterprises, in the inconvertibility of the currency, in the low effectiveness of capital investment, and in the social perception of the illegitimacy of communist rule that contributed to poor work motivation. Thus, Poland became economically bankrupt in the middle of the 1970s. Loans became very difficult to procure, and Polish goods did not have access to western markets, both because of their low quality and because of the economic recession in West Europe.

The economic crisis and growing social tensions in the middle of the 1970s demanded new solutions. Again, to a certain extent, as in the time of NEP, a new strategy was desperately needed to survive. Social pressure for improved living conditions, a lack of easy ways of increasing production, and foreign debts contributed to crises that, after several years, forced a more flexible policy in many areas of economic and social life.

III. CHANGES IN FORMAL RULES FOR FORMATION OF JOINT VENTURES WITH FOREIGN CAPITAL IN POLAND

Almost all communist countries have permitted foreign capital for a direct investment on their territories. Yugoslavia started in 1967, Romania joined in 1971, then followed Hungary in 1972, Poland in 1976, China in 1979, Bulgaria in 1980, and more recently, Czechoslovakia in 1986, and the Soviet Union on January 13, 1987. These dates show how relatively new this phenomenon is in international economic relations.

Advocates of a new policy emphasized that joint activity with foreign investors on the territory of communist countries provides an opportunity for the concentration of factors of development such as capital, productive capacities, technology, and managerial expertise. In this way, partners make possible the completion of projects far beyond their own individual potential (Burzynski 1987).

Looking at Polish legislation from a historical standpoint, we see three regulations appearing at the same time:

1. Decree of the Council of Ministers of May 14, 1976, concerning the issuance of permits to foreign legal and natural persons for conducting various types of economic activity;[3]
2. Decree of the Minister of Finance of May 26, 1976, permitting the opening and use of bank accounts for those who conduct economic activity in Poland;[4] and
3. Decree of the Minister of Finance of May 26, 1976, concerning permits for foreign exchange operations by mixed capital companies.

This new set of rules created the potential for the access of foreign capital to the Polish economy. However, it was only a limited opening. Only a few areas—such as crafts, retail trade, catering, hotels, and other minor services—were designated for foreign investment. In 1978, the regulations were extended to include all manufacturing and service activities. According to an amendment issued December 1, 1978,[5] a permit for a foreign enterprise could be granted for a period longer than ten years if justified by the nature of the economic activity, the value of the investment, and the projected investment return. Local administrators in 50 offices throughout the country were in charge of issuing permits. Prior to obtaining a permit, a foreign investor had to present a cost projection for the investment, a commitment to cover the full cost of the investment in convertible currency, and a bank certificate proving that 30 percent of the estimated investment cost had been deposited in convertible currency.

3. *Monitor Polski*, No. 25, Item 109.
4. *Monitor Polski*, No. 25, Item 110.
5. *Journal of Laws*, No. 13, Item 138.

This Decree of the Minister of Finance was a significant step for the development of joint ventures because it provided an opportunity for establishing mixed capital companies in Poland. According to its provisions, foreign legal persons or associations of Poles living abroad could enter into an agreement with Polish state enterprises, cooperatives, or nonprofit organizations for conducting business activities in the form of a mixed capital company. In that case, the Minister of Finance and the minister responsible for the given branch of the national economy were in charge of issuing appropriate permits. A necessary capital contribution of the foreign partner had to be made in Polish currency, obtained from a documented exchange of convertible currency. Nonpecuniary contributions were also allowed, but for no more than 50 percent of the total contribution. In both cases, wholly owned and mixed, foreign partners could receive part of their profits in convertible currency, although in a given tax year only 9 percent of the value of the capital contributed by the foreign partner was allowed to be converted into hard currency. This latter restriction did not apply if 50 percent or more of the profit was generated by the export goods or services.

The Decree of 1976 marked a good beginning to the next important steps, but it did not accomplish any significant achievements in itself. Neither side, foreign investors as well as governmental agencies and local authorities in Poland, was prepared to understand the complicated issue of a communist system on the one hand, and the rules of the market on the other.

Four major decrees and resolutions established in the spring of 1979 were the next steps toward an open economy:

1. Resolution of the Council of Ministers of February 7, 1979, on Establishing Business Enterprises with Foreign Capital Participation in Poland, and their Operations;[6]
2. Decree of the Minister of Foreign Trade and Maritime Economy of March 28, 1979, on the Permission to Conduct Certain Foreign Trade Activities by Foreign Corporate Bodies and Individuals;[7]

---

6. *Monitor Polski,* No. 10, Item 67.
7. *Monitor Polski,* No. 10, Item 68.

3. Decree of the Minister of Labor, Wages, and Social Benefits of
    May 30, 1979, regarding Some Principles of Employment and
    Compensation of the Employees of Limited Liability
    Companies with Foreign Participation;[8] and
4. Decree of the Minister of Finance of June 18, 1979, Concerning
    Financial Operations of Business Enterprises with Foreign
    Capital Participation and on Permits for Conducting Certain
    Foreign Exchange Operations.[9]

As one of the most outstanding advocates for joint ventures, Dr.
A. Burzyniski emphasized the fact that the main act, the Resolution
on Establishing Business Enterprises with Foreign Capital
Participation in Poland and their Operations, was issued by the
Council of Ministers, not the Minister of Finance, as previously
was the most important feature of the new set of regulations. The
Council of Ministers is the highest authority of the government of
Poland, which means that a resolution was issued by the whole
government, and that other branches and functional ministers
had to follow it. We must remember that coordination is extremely difficult in a government where particular ministers gov-
ern over very separate, limited areas of the economy and public
matters. If the Minister of Finance issued a decree, for instance,
the message would be that his office was interested in increasing
exports and hard currency earnings, which some of his colleagues
would see as irrelevant to their actions. Regulations issued by one
minister, even when regarding the entire economy, were often
not followed by others in the government.

Due to its legal status, the new set of rules sent the message to
foreign investors that the government was willing to attract foreign capital and wanted to achieve some progress on that issue. In
terms of their appeal to foreign investors, however, the new regulations did not bring many significant changes and required even
more detailed procedures for permit applications.

The application was to be submitted by a managing director of a
state enterprise or by a president of a cooperative. A special statement was required from the relevant Polish foreign trade agency

8. *Monitor Polski*, No. 15, Item 88.
9. *Monitor Polski*, No. 16, Item 97.

concerning the prospects for future export of the joint venture's products to convertible currency markets.   The new regulations limited the scope of activities of the prospective joint venture to that allowed to cooperatives and small industrial organizations under the authority of a regional public administration, which meant that only small and medium-scale organizations, functioning outside of central priorities, could be involved in joint ventures with foreign capital. Permits for remission of convertible currency were to be issued only within the limits of the convertible currency reserves of the last joint venture.

The regulations of 1979 shared their limited effectiveness with the acts of 1976. They had very limited impact on the Polish economy.   A number of wholly owned small foreign businesses were established in that time, but because of their separation from the mainstream of the Polish economy, they did not play a significant role. Despite this, they have been the subject of dogmatic debate regarding social justice, wages, equity, and other ideological issues.

The next step in the regulation of foreign investment was made in 1982.   It consisted of two laws established by the Polish Parliament: the Law on Banking of February 16, 1982,[10] and the Law on Foreign Corporate Bodies and Natural Person's Economic Activity in Poland.[11] These regulations were not novel in their content, but the fact that they had been issued by Parliament changed the position of the issue of foreign investment not only in the economy but also in the political system.   Now, we have regulation acts that are supposed to be followed by enterprises as well as by the government and its agencies; it is the highest level of authority possible in a business law.   It is under these rules that more than half of the 840 foreign-owned companies currently in operation were established.

The next step in the evolution was undertaken by the Parliament in 1986, with the passage of the Law on Companies with Foreign Capital Participation of April 12, 1986.[12] This time it was a specific joint-venture law. Thus, a ten-year period of evolu-

---

10. *Dziennik Ustaw*, No. 7, Item 56.
11. *Op. cit.*
12. *Dziennik Ustaw*, No. 17, Item 88.

tion of regulation regarding foreign investment in the Polish economy was closed.

At least two contradictions regarding the nature of a joint venture as a business organization should be noted in regard to this new law. The first is the political status of a joint venture with foreign capital, and the second is the one-dimensional, pro-export focus of the law. According to Article 26, Item 1, joint ventures with foreign capital participate in the economy in the same way as other businesses, whether they are state-owned or cooperative. State enterprises are called "socialized units of the economy" in the official political language. In relationships with other organizations in the Polish economy and with governmental agencies, joint ventures were regulated through the laws and resolutions that every business is obliged to follow, if the Law on Companies with Foreign Capital Participation does not prescribe some other way. The location of joint ventures in the economic system resulted in many negative consequences that were criticized by Polish (Rajski 1986) as well as foreign researchers (Juergensmeyer 1987).

The difficult economic situation in Poland, the centralized management system, and the too-often changing regulations regarding the economy created a climate that discouraged foreigners to invest and form larger businesses. Article 32, Item 2 says that Polish law determines the compensation of employees, insurance, and other issues in joint-venture operations. The role itself was quite obvious, but a specific regulation that followed it contributed to many management problems. There were several taxes that joint ventures, as well as other socialized units of the economy, had to pay. Let us take as an example employee compensation. At that time, every state-owned firm had to pay a special tax when it wanted to increase employees' wages above a certain level paid in the previous year. In a market economy, an entrepreneur is free to increase the wages of employees due to their higher productivity or to increase prices for his goods on the market place.

In the Polish economy of 1987, the following scenario was possible: a wage increase above 12 percent of the 1986 level would cost an enterprise a tax equal to 500 percent of the excess wage increase. However, this did not mean that every enterprise would pay 500 percent in such a situation. There were hundreds of exceptions, due to the five different rules regulating the issue and the individual bargaining of managers with the state agencies. This additional tax on wages was designed to prevent excessive wage increases that would contribute to a higher rate of inflation. Simultaneously, higher wages would decrease enterprise profit, decreasing, as a result, government revenues as well. For many reasons, this mechanism did not work. Wages and prices of goods were growing excessively, simply because of the political nature of economic processes in a communist state. Wages have always been a political issue in communism. Growth of wages to create an impression of improved well-being was a very well-established strategy practiced by the government to maintain social peace for as long as possible. There are still some elements of that strategy in current government actions.

In sum, the tax was implemented in an effort to develop an effectiveness of the economy at a micro level. The problem is that, due to heavy taxation, enterprises had very limited investment funds, even if they were successful. Joint ventures were in the same boat, but in a much worse position. While fully state-owned enterprises were granted subventions, tax holidays, and other forms of budgetary support to maintain their employment and wage increases, joint ventures, as partially foreign-owned units, did not enjoy such special treatment. The repressive taxes mentioned above did not allow for the free allocation of resources inside an enterprise according to the best possible profit they would generate. There was no opportunity to minimize wage costs per unit of production without an additional tax penalty. An increase of individual wages was virtually impossible without incurring a tax penalty, but with the increase the development of the firm was hardly possible.

The Fund of Foreign Debts was another difficult problem. This tax was established as 2 percent of the value of production volume counted at the end of the previous year; it was intended to help defray the cost of foreign debts. The tax was supposed to be withdrawn from a portion of the profit reserved for business development. It was a controversial question whether or not a joint venture that did not contribute to the development of Polish debts should suffer a diminution of opportunities in order to reduce the state's debts.

Another controversial issue concerned the income tax. According to Article 30, Item 1, this tax is paid from verified profit earned in the previous year and is increased by costs and waste

considered unacceptable by order of the Polish Council of
Ministers. What constitutes unacceptable costs? The definition of
an unacceptable cost differed according to the orders of the Council
of Ministers. The idea of an unacceptable cost was implemented to
prevent inefficient practices in enterprises. When a company's
profits are not of the desired value, but there is no competition or
market demand is greater than supply, it is quite easy to lose an
economic approach to business. To maintain pressures for minimizing costs rather than simply raising output prices, the government established the concept of unacceptable costs. Of course, managers learned to rename particular costs to avoid such punishment.
For business people operating in market-type conditions, this idea
and its implementation through changeable rules issued by the
Council of Ministers may appear strange. For Polish firms, it created insecurity because profit was unknown until it was reviewed.

Joint ventures treated as socialized units of the economy had to
pay regular taxes, some examples of which were mentioned above.
All such taxes contributed to price increases and limited market
demand. Higher prices did not necessarily mean increased profits. Sometimes more than 40 percent of the price was absorbed by
taxes, and the profits obtained in this manner flowed to the state.

The second set of problems concerns the strong pressure to export
goods by a joint venture with foreign capital. According to governmental policy, export was assumed to be an ultimate goal of
joint ventures with foreign capital. This assumption was followed
by numerous incentives for export for hard currency. For example,
the profits of joint ventures were taxed at a rate of 50 percent, which
is 15 percent lower than in other socialized units of the economy,
but each zloty of exports in relation to the total value of goods
resulted in a decrease of 0.4 percent in the tax. If a company exported every good it produced, the tax would be lowered to 10
percent. Another strong incentive for export was included in the
tax on gross sales. Goods and services exported were free from this
type of tax, encouraging exports for hard currency but significantly
reducing the economic rationality of many business transactions.

In this way, the law of 1986 and earlier provisions build incon-
sistency into the joint-venture concept. Joint ventures as a vehicle
for hard currency earnings, as well as joint ventures as business
investment for maximization of profit over a long period, were in

conflict under these rules. The existing rules prevented long-term commitment. The limited period during which a company was permitted to operate, and the limited rights for selling ownership to another person or company, even to family of the current owner, reinforced the short-term orientation of joint ventures.

The system of permits also created monopolistic structures. Rights to establish joint ventures were granted according to the definition of the needs of the economy made by the government rather than by the market. Newcomers were incorporated into the old structures and governed by old rules, a situation that resulted in economic disaster and social crisis.

IV. THE LAW ON ECONOMIC ACTIVITY WITH FOREIGN CAPITAL PARTICIPATION OF 1989

After several years of discussions with management professionals, foreign investors, and government agencies, Parliament established a new law for regulating joint ventures in Poland. In an introduction to specific rules two goals were emphasized: (1) the stabilization of economic collaboration between foreign and Polish companies, and (2) a government guarantee of foreigners' property rights. The new law is the most comprehensive and liberal regulation on joint ventures in the communist bloc. It still has some elements of the previous regulations, but it successfully shapes a new framework for foreign investment and creates much more secure and liberal conditions for joint economic activities. First, we will describe the incentives and requirements established by the new law, and then we will compare the new rules to the law of 1986. By means of this comparison, we will see how significantly different the new law is from previous regulations.

Incentives for Foreign Investment in Joint Ventures

1. There are no taxes for the first three years.
2. An additional three years of tax-free operation is granted.
3. A foreign shareholder can obtain a compensation payment guarantee to the amount equal to the value of a company's assets.

This sum is payable to the foreign investor in the event of a loss resulting from a decision of the state authorities regarding nationalization, expropriation, or measures having an effect equivalent to nationalization or expropriation.

4. A foreign shareholder has the right of transfer profit abroad without a foreign exchange permit.
5. No permit is necessary for the use of foreign exchange to purchase goods and services abroad.
6. The corporate income tax is 40 percent of taxable income.
7. The corporate income tax rate decreases by 0.4 percent for each percentage point of the share of export turnover in total turnover after the deduction of turnover tax.

Requirements for Formation of Joint Ventures with Foreign Capital

1. A permit for a joint venture is necessary.
2. A permit shall be denied without any explanation whenever business activity may result in a threat to the state's economic or security and defense interests or in a violation of environmental protection laws.
3. The decision to deny a permit may not be appealed to the court.
4. Regulations pertaining to socialized units of the economy are not applicable to joint ventures with foreign capital unless the law states otherwise.
5. Raw material supply in the domestic market is regulated by rules applicable to socialized units of the economy.
6. The transfer of shares of ownership within the company among shareholders requires a special permit.
7. An amendment to the company's founding act that changes the ratio of equity holdings, the related voting rights, or the nature of the value of the partners' contributions requires a special permit.
8. The acquisition of shares by a new person requires a special permit.
9. A change in the object of the company's activity, as specified in the permit, requires a special permit.
10. The distribution of profit among shareholders based on other than their holdings in the company requires a special permit.

Table 8-1. Comparison of Joint-Venture Laws of 1986 and 1989

Element	1986 Law	1989 Law
Permission Required to Enter a JV	From Several Agencies	From One Agency
JV's Status in the Economy	Socialized Unit of the Economy	Nonsocialized Unit of the Economy
Ownership Rights	Limited	Limited
Ratio of Equities	Frozen	Frozen
Freedom of Allocation of Resources within Company	Restricted	Controlled
Freedom of Allocation within Economy	Restricted	Regulated
Foreign Investment	Maximum 49 Percent	Minimum 20 Percent
Transfer of Currency	Regulated	Unrestricted
Obligatory Sale of Hard Currency	25 Percent of Exports	15 Percent of Exports
Taxes	Like Socialized Units	Like Private Firms
Income Tax	40 Percent	40 Percent
Tax-Free	Two Years	Three Years
Tax Reduction	For Export	For Export
Investment Guarantee	Not Guaranteed	Guaranteed

11. A company shall sell 15 percent of its foreign currency export income to a Polish foreign exchange bank.
12. Foreign investors may have not less than 20 percent of equity, but they must have a minimum investment of US$50,000.
13. The following taxes, the same as those applied to socialized units of the economy but with lower rates, are imposed on joint ventures: the turnover real estate tax, the corporate income tax, the agricultural tax (-40 percent), the wage tax (-30 percent), local municipal taxes, and stamp duties. This law marks significant progress in the liberalization of requirements. Such a liberalization is visible when we compare the current regulations with the law of 1986, as we do in Table 8-1.

The most significant difference between these two sets of rules is in the new philosophy of regulation, employed in 1989. Foreign participation is required to a minimum of 20 percent of investment, in contrast to the previous regulation where only a maximum on the western share of investment was established. In all important dimensions, the new regulation provides a more liberal and more convenient framework for foreign investment. According to foreign entrepreneurs (Lewandowski 1989) conducting business in Poland, almost all weaknesses of the previous regulation were removed. One exception is the lack of written assurance of stability. An important weakness of business regulation in communist countries is its changeability and the continuous experiments in taxes and management. Uncertainty over business conditions, legal rules, required accounting procedures, and other guidelines made business operation difficult and unpredictable. The new law reflects the government's intention to stabilize the legal framework of joint ventures, but it does not guarantee them to business people expecting, say, 50 years of stability of regulations. Nonetheless, as we mentioned in the beginning, four months' experience with the new law has resulted in a tremendous growth of joint ventures.

V. CONCLUSIONS

An evolution of regulations regarding foreign investment in the Polish economy illustrates a process of change that sooner or later

all other communist countries will experience. Today, these processes are advanced in Hungary, while the Soviet Union is on the
same path. Two very important features of the evolution of Polish
rules for foreign investment are that joint ventures with foreign
capital gradually moved from state control to private busi-ness, and
that fully foreign-owned companies were finally permitted. A
market economy in Poland is still far from reality, but the effort
for its creation exists, and many social forces are engaged in the
endeavor. A new Polish government dominated by Solidarity is
the best guarantee of the continuity of these changes.

REFERENCES

Bobrowski, C. Z. 1946. Przmowienie na XI Sesji KRN.

Brus, W., and M. Pohorille. 1953a. Zagadnienia Budowy Ekono-
micznych Podstaw Socjalizmu. Warsaw.

——. 1953b. Okres Przcjsciowy od Kapitalizmu so Socializmu.
Warsaw.

Brzezinski, B., and J. Gluchowski. 1987. "Regulaeje Finansowc
Winowym Prawie o Spolkach z Udzialem Zagranicznym."
Panstwo i Prawo, May.

Burzynski, A. 1987. "Evolution of Polish Investment Law." Paper
present at the Forum for Promotion of Joint Ventures, UNIDO,
Warsaw, October 12-15.

Burkhardt, A. 1982. "Promotion of East-West Joint Ventures by
Governments of Western Countries." *International Business
Lawyer*, October.

Bukharin, N. 1934. *Imperialism a Gospodarka Siwiatowa*. Warsaw.

Buzescu, P. 1984. "Joint Ventures in Eastern Europe." *American
Journal of Comparative Law*, April.

Juergensmeyer, J. C. 1987. "Perspective on the Prospect for Joint
Ventures as New Form of Cooperation Between East and West."
Paper presented at the Forum for Promotion of Joint Ventures,
UNIDO, Warsaw, October 12-15.

Lange, O. 1957. *O Niektorych Zagadnicniach Polskiej Drogi do
Socjalizmu*. Warsaw.

Lis, K. 1987. "Joint Venture Management Problems." Paper presented at the Forum for Promotion of Joint Ventures, UNIDO, Warsaw, October 12-15.

Lewandowski, Z. 1989. Interesy z Polska, Przekroj, May 17.

Iwanowska, A., and H. Sterniczuk. 1989. "Legal and Political Environment of Entrepreneurship and New Entrepreneurs in Poland." Paper. The Academy of Management, Washington, DC.

Janiszewski, H. 1989. W Grudniu Bedzie Piecset, Zycie Gospodarcze, August 27.

Kozinski, J. 1987. "Joint Ventures in Poland—Case Study Formula." Paper presented at the Forum for Promotion of Joint Ventures, UNIDO, Warsaw, October 12-15.

Malecki, N. 1987. "The Conditions of Foreign Capital Functioning in Socialist Countries—A Comparative Study." Paper presented at the Forum for Promotion of Joint Ventures, UNIDO, Warsaw, October 12-15.

Malenkow, G. 1952. Referat na XIX Zjazd KC WKP(b).

Minc, H. 1946. O Przejeciu na Wlasnosc Panstwa Podstawowych Galezi Gospodarki Narodowej. Lodz.

Rajski, I. 1986. "Nowe Prawo o Spolkach z Udzialem Zagranicznym." Panstwo i Prawo, November.

Scriven, J. 1982. "Co-operation in East-West Trade: The Equity Joint Venture." International Business Lawyer, October.

Stalin, J. 1952. Ekonomiczne Problemy Socjalizmu w ZSRR, Warsaw.

Financial and Capital Market Reform

CHAPTER 9

The Soviet Credit and Enterprise Structure System Under Reform

VLADIMIR MUSATOV

Radical Soviet economic reform will transform the entire economy, including the credit system. Although several reforms are
in the experimental stage and many problems remain, the transition to a new, more efficient credit system in the Soviet Union has
begun. Decentralization is one of the main trends in the development of the Soviet credit system, and it could be said that decentralization in this sector of the economy has made more progress
than in others. This paper briefly addresses two related problems:
(1) banking reform, and (2) the issuance of stock by Soviet enterprises, which is firmly connected to the enterprise's organizational structure.

BANKING REFORM: A NEW PHASE AHEAD?

Banking reform, clearly one of the most important developments
in economic reform, has gone almost unnoticed by the general
public. Nevertheless, the foundation for the new banking system
has been laid, and, apart from the Gosbank, five so-called
"specialized banks" have been created. The state entrusted these
state banks with servicing corresponding spheres of the economy.
The creation of commercial banks, from very small ones with capital of 1 million rubles to large ones having several million rubles,
has also been allowed. Such banks have already been established

by cooperatives, regional unions of cooperatives, enterprises in the same industry (such as the chemical and construction industries), and single large concerns (such as "Energomash," one of the first concerns based in Leningrad).

In the pre-perestroika period, the enterprises were given capital based on the system of centralized allocation of new capital investments.   Thus, the banking system's credit resources were distributed among various projects according to decisions made by central economic bodies.   Since the new commercial banks are not bound by the planning decisions made by others, they can make their own investment decisions.   Previously, the branches of the two main banks were obliged to finance enterprises and collective farms that were deeply in the red, or to finance construction projects with extremely long construction times.   Managers of the banks' branches usually realized the unsound nature of the loans they extended, but the prerogatives of the branches, and in most cases those of the banks' headquarters themselves, were extremely limited.   Although the "specialized banks" to a large extent inherited this feature, the commercial banks did not.   New financial instruments and new types of financial institutions will tend to enhance the differentiation among enterprises.   Those that are better off will attract external funds to expand their activities, while those that are already deeply indebted will struggle to remain afloat.

And so a new element, competition, was introduced into the banking system.   So far, the opportunities for commercial banks to compete are rather limited, but the first step, always the most difficult, has been taken.   The direction was taken, and it can be expected that the scope of competition will grow.

The new commercial banks will, by speeding up the differentiation among enterprises, make the need to solve the problem of unprofitable enterprises even more pressing.   This, in turn, will eventually place the credit system on a more sound base and diminish inflationary pressures.

Because they have the ability to make independent investment decisions, the new banks will automatically try to diversify their assets to diminish the risk.   In the distant future, this will raise for the largest of them the question of international diversification. The first step, financing of joint ventures in the Soviet Union, could be taken rather soon. Undoubtedly, the new banks will establish relations with joint ventures even if they now lack the ability to provide hard currency loans to their clients.

It would be wrong, however, to assume that the mushrooming of commercial banks has only positive consequences. One of the major dangers connected with the appearance of new financial intermediaries is the tendency of some banks to retain the present economic structure built strictly along branch lines. Branch ministries are strongly criticized, and some of them have already been disbanded due to the formation of still larger ministries consisting of two or three such former entities. But ministries now might receive an unexpected helping hand from commercial banks organized to serve the enterprises of a single industry. Almost by definition, such banks will be among the potentially powerful tools at the disposal of the ministries because the ministries initiate their formation. Furthermore, such banks are formed under the auspices of the respective ministries. High-ranking ministry officials might receive dominant or influential positions in the body controlling the activities of the bank. In such a case, the bank formed by the enterprises of one industry (and formed to serve this industry) might strengthen the monopoly position of the ministry, especially if the goods supplied by this industry are in short supply.

Such banks might pressure their clients to make lopsided deals. Let us consider a hypothetical, though by no means purely theoretical, case. A bank belonging to an important industry producing, say, machine tools, wants to expand its lending base and decides to issue additional shares. But it searches for prospective new shareholders only among those in need of machine tools, offering them a deal that nobody would even consider seriously in conventional circumstances: the buyers of the shares will not receive any dividends, nor will they have voting rights, but in exchange the bank will help them to acquire the necessary machine tools. In a deficit-ridden economy, it would be only natural for the buyers to agree. By the same token, the allocation of funds would continue to be distorted. And what is even worse, the commercial bank, supposedly a new financial institution that should help the restructuring of the economy, hinders the progress of reform.

On a brighter note, the effectiveness of the credit system will be enhanced by the specialization of the new institutions. For example, it can be predicted easily that many of the new financial institutions will specialize primarily in providing funds for housing construction. Several such institutions have already appeared. They are quasi-banks in essence, even though they might be called something very different. A good example is a small (like all of them) institution, called rather confusingly a "credit and clearing center," that functions in one of the Russian Federation's autonomous republics. It was organized by several construction companies to finance housing construction mostly for those employed in the companies. People bought shares issued by the center. The proceeds were used to finance the construction of a building with 100 apartments. Upon completion of the project, the apartments were sold to those who could afford them, and the center switched to another housing project. The shareholders received dividends amounting to 7 percent annually.

One of the main problems plaguing the commercial banks is the low number of experienced people with a background in banking.

The need to continue banking reform becomes clear. First, the Gosbank should be firmly placed in the middle of the banking system as a full-fledged central bank. Second, the scope of competition should be increased, and "specialized banks" should lose the privileges that place commercial banks at a disadvantage. And finally, commercial banks should be better regulated by the central bank.

TOWARD THE FORMATION OF A SECURITIES MARKET

Stock ownership and issuing stock to raise equity capital are not alien to the socialist economy in either theory or practice. Nor are securities a totally novel concept for the Soviet economy. In the 1920s, a wide range of securities was issued, primarily different kinds of bonds. Even the stock exchanges were resurrected in several cities as departments at commodity exchanges. When at the end of the 1920s the whole course of economic development was abruptly changed, the issuance of securities for enterprises was prohibited, and markets for securities, as well as for commodities, were closed.

The state retained the right to issue bonds and used it extensively, especially after World War II. In those years, government bonds were like an additional (and heavy) tax. Wage and salary earners were in fact obliged to subscribe to a certain portion of bonds that had to be placed among the personnel of the enterprise. Bonds bought by an individual worker during a year could have amounted to two months' income. This practice was stopped in the 1950s, but it turned out that the government lacked the financial resources to cover its obligations to bondholders. And so, the repayment of the principal was postponed for several years. The question of interest payments, as if it did not exist, was not even raised. Even now, a relatively small amount of those bonds still has not been redeemed, though the majority of them were repaid.

This unfortunate saga clearly discredited the whole concept of bonds in the eyes of many Soviet citizens. From an economic and organizational point of view, it is better to begin anew with the creation of a bond market and only after that to proceed with a stock market. Whereas Hungary, for example, took exactly this path, the Soviet Union has decided to begin with shares. It appears that many officials, given the legacy of past decades, believe that the stocks will be psychologically more acceptable than bonds. But, psychology aside, developments have their own logic that often dictates the sequence of events. Stocks happened to be the first to enter the market, but they have been given many characteristics typical of bonds.

It should be stressed that the initiative to issue stock was firmly seized by enterprises, both industrial and agricultural. They began to issue stock *before* the government decided how to organize the whole process. There was a desire on the part of the enterprises to order a batch of stock, so to speak, in the nearby printing shop. In fact, several enterprises did exactly that. Official documents regulating stock issues were published in the fall of 1988, as the government tried to catch up with what was happening in this sphere of the economy.

Two kinds of securities, literally called "shares of enterprise" and "shares of the labor collective," were authorized. Their most important common feature is that neither gives voting rights to their holders.   In an attempt to make the allocation of financial resources more efficient, stock of the first kind can be bought only by enterprises.   Enterprises with plenty of cash can acquire stock of other enterprises and thereby receive a more substantial income in the form of dividends than that the often symbolic interest banks pay on deposits.   For their part, the issuers of stocks can use the proceeds to finance their investment projects.

But it can be argued that in an economy notorious for shortages of investment goods, financial resources are in many cases the least important problem.   Many enterprises have accumulated substantial funds but cannot find the investment goods.   On the other hand, there are other enterprises that are in the red and are in need of financial resources.   But it would be difficult to expect the appearance of many enthusiastic buyers for their stock.

The second type of stock, which exists to motivate workers, can be distributed only to enterprise employees.   Dividend payments can be both floating and fixed.   The securities can be issued for a stated number of years.   Such a scheme is not free of problems, however. Unequal distribution of financial resources owned by individuals in different regions of the country could be exacerbated if stocks are sold freely.   And it would be wrong to give to those who already own unearned (criminal activities included) money the chance to increase their unearned income further (legally this time).

A variety of restrictions exists on the acquisition of stocks issued to personnel.   The quantity of shares acquired by one person cannot exceed the maximum value of stocks set by the enterprise labor collective.   This value is often limited to 10,000 rubles (this sum approximately equals the average wage for four years).   Finally, it is up to the labor collective to decide whether all employees, or only those who have worked for several years, are eligible to become shareholders.

The movement of stocks is restricted as well.   They must be surrendered to the enterprise when a person quits.   Employees have no right to sell them to a third party.   Redemption by the enterprise is the only possibility.   In the case of retirement, the worker may be given the right to hold stocks and to receive dividends, but a corresponding decision of the labor collective's council is needed, with the outcome depending on the employee's record.   Moreover, the amount of dividends received by individual shareholders may

to some extent depend—if such a rule is adopted at the enterprise—
on the employee's record during the period for which the dividend is paid. For example, the shareholder might receive less
than others if in the corresponding period of time he or she was
guilty of absenteeism.

Stock and Agriculture

Stocks issued in the agricultural sector deserve special consideration. Rather peculiar forms of dividend payments are practiced by
some issuers in the agricultural sector. Instead of cash, the shareholders (they make the choice themselves) can receive, for example, foodstuffs. It makes sense because of the shortage of such items
in many places.

There could be reasons to judge as a relatively important phenomenon the issuance of stocks by collective farms. Actually, several collective farms were among the first to issue stocks. They
rushed to do it even before the government officially allowed this
practice and established the rules.

In the discussions now under way, many criticize the collective
farm as a form of agricultural enterprise. And there are those who
believe that collective farms have no future and should be disbanded. Oddly, however, those who defend the viability of the collective farm usually do not mention the issuance of stocks, the factor
that may unexpectedly be one of the most prominent. Formally,
the members of a collective farm always were co-owners of the
farm, and their income depended on the proceeds of the whole
farm. But only formally. The size of the remuneration and the
ways in which it was distributed deprived the collective farmer of
the motivation to work hard. New tools are badly needed; stocks
may become one of them. Of course, it is difficult to say if the issuance of stocks can help those collective farms called
"millionaires," only because their debts have reached millions of
rubles. Probably not, because in many cases it is next to impossible
to turn such farms around (even if their debts are annulled by the
state). It could be a completely different story with prosperous collective farms, or those that have the potential to become prosperous,
if offering stock turns out to be an efficient way to motivate mem-

bers.   The collective farmer who is a shareholder will become much more active in all matters concerning the development of the farm.

Let us take the example of a very successful collective farm in Lithuania.   It distributed among its members ownership of 40 percent of its assets in the form of stock.   Now each member of the farm (excluding those who worked less than six years) has a valuable financial asset and is directly interested in its growth, that is, in its profitability.   Part of the profits are distributed as dividends. Last year, their value exceeded 50 percent of annual wages.   This clearly gives the shareholders the sense of receiving a sizeable part of their income on the property they own.   Such dividends are far from symbolic and can effectively motivate the shareholders.[1]

Agriculture aside, broader problems concerning stock are of primary importance.   It is notable that, in many instances, enterprises that issued stock began to call themselves "corporations." From the point of view of laws now in force, this is totally unfounded.   The official documents firmly state that the status of an enterprise does not change after it issues stock.

Another phenomenon worth mentioning is the amazing speed with which the idea to issue stock—real stock that gives voting power—is gaining popularity.   Perestroika is widely known as a revolution from above.   But as far as stock is concerned, the initiative is still in the hands of the enterprises.[2]

The conceptual point of view expressed in this paper clearly manifests the desirability (to put it mildly) of transforming the majority of Soviet enterprises into corporations.

Organizational Reform

Such a transition should be considered truly urgent.   The Soviet economy now needs measures characterized simultaneously by

---

1. Of course, shares might be used in agriculture not only by collective farms, and used more efficiently than now, when shares in general lack one of the main characteristics: voting power.

2. Incidentally, not the largest ones in the beginning.   But now the giants are catching up.

three features: (1) the ability to provide results relatively swiftly; (2) the ability to be multifunctional, serving several needs; and (3) the ability to guarantee against undesirable side effects, and not only those that outweigh the positive results.

The incorporation of Soviet enterprises should be seen as one of the main steps in the radical economic reform. It must be implemented as soon as possible because it combines all three features mentioned above. In this respect, it differs greatly from price reform or the introduction of cooperatives. Price reform is badly needed, but it must be postponed because of prohibitive social costs. The cooperatives brought with them menacing side effects when they aroused anger among a considerable part of the population. The potential economic role of the incorporation of Soviet enterprises can be summarized as comprising the following five functions:

1. It will greatly help to restructure the economy and to achieve the structural changes needed to make the economy more susceptible to technological progress and innovation. Enterprises will enter into different kinds of combinations with each other according to their needs and disregard the artificial "boundaries" imposed by ministries that divided the economy into narrow branches. Multidivisional, diversified companies will become the backbone of the economy instead of today's enterprises, which belong to one branch and consist of one factory.

   The transition should be more or less simultaneous. Shares (in the proper sense of the word, not a surrogate) should be issued if not by all then definitely by the absolute majority of enterprises. That is why such a transformation cannot be viewed as a voluntary act—enterprises should be obliged to issue shares.

   Individual ownership of the means of production will not be reinstated in the Soviet Union as a dominant feature of the economy (although it will probably reappear and occupy some place in the economic life). Individuals will not have the possibility to control corporations through the ownership of shares. But it does not mean that they should be completely excluded from holding the voting shares.

There are enterprises that should be wholly owned by the state. In other cases, the state will retain the majority of the shares or a substantial block of them. And the majority of enterprises will freely sell their stock and exchange it with other enterprises. It can be predicted that the exchange of stock will at the beginning happen more often.

2. The issuing of stock will make the allocation of financial resources more efficient. This mechanism will work properly after stock has been given voting power.

3. The network of stock ownership will cement the new type of relationship between enterprises. Administrative centralization will be replaced by a "new centralization" based on the economic relations between large concerns and small and medium-sized enterprises.

4. Stocks will be a powerful tool for the long-term motivation of personnel. Pensions guaranteed by the state should be supplemented by the income accumulated during the employee's career. The responsibility of the individual employee for his or her financial position after retirement will be increased.

5. The incorporation of Soviet enterprises will enhance the possibilities to increase external economic relations. The exchange of stock, for example, with foreign companies can be envisioned as one of the methods to strengthen cooperation between the partners. Sooner or later, the question of shares issued abroad will arise.

The obvious first candidates to issue stock abroad are the joint ventures. One difficulty they will meet should be especially stressed: many joint ventures are created for a limited period, sometimes as short as five years and rarely as long as 25 years.

CONCLUSION

It should be repeated that the incorporation of Soviet enterprises will accelerate positive changes in the economy.

One remark has to be made on the issue of introducing stock exchanges. This issue was not discussed in this paper, although it is often raised.   First of all, there should be equities in the proper sense of the word that could be traded on the exchanges. After incorporation, the problem of the specific form the securities market will take will be resolved quickly.   It does not significantly matter whether or not there will be stock exchanges.   Of primary importance is that the securities market will automatically appear after the incorporation of the enterprises.   And one aspect is totally clear: the securities market should be computerized from the beginning.   If there is a stock exchange, it should be an automatic one.

INDEX

ABOUT THE CONTRIBUTORS

ALEXANDER BELOV is Research Fellow at the Soviet Institute for the Study of the USA and Canada.

JOZEF M. VAN BRABANT is Chief of Centrally Planned Economies at the United Nations

ROBERT V. DANIELS is Professor Emeritus of History at the University of Vermont.

ALEXEI KUNITSIN is Senior Research Fellow at the Soviet Institute for the Study of the USA and Canada.

MARIE LAVIGNE is Professor of Economics at the University of Paris I Pantheon-Sorbonne, and Director of the Center for International Economics of Socialist Countries at the University of Paris.

KRZYSZTOF A. LIS is Polish Minister for Privatization, and Professor at the School of Management at Warsaw University.

KALMAN MIZSEI is Senior Fellow at the Institute for World Economics, Hungarian Academy of Sciences.

VLADIMIR MUSATOV is Head of the Economics Department at the Soviet Institute for the Study of the USA and Canada.

SCOTT PARDEE is Chairman of Yamaichi International America, Inc.

ALEXANDER PARKANSKY is Senior Research Fellow at the Soviet Institute for the Study of the USA and Canada.

VLADIMIR POPOV is Senior Research Fellow at the Soviet Institute for the Study of the USA and Canada.

FRANCIS SCOTLAND is Senior Partner at Bank Credit Analysts, Ltd.

HENRYK STERNICZUK is Professor, Division of Administration, at the University of New Brunswick, Saint John, Canada.

ABOUT THE EDITORS

JOSEF C. BRADA is Professor of Economics at Arizona State University. After having received both a B.S. in chemical engineering and an M.A. in economics from Tufts University, Dr. Brada went on to receive a Ph.D. in economics from the University of Minnesota. He is currently the Editor of the *Journal of Comparative Economics*, and is a member of the Board of Trustees for the National Council for Soviet and East European Research.

MICHAEL P. CLAUDON is President and Managing Director of the Geonomics Institute, and Professor of Economics at Middlebury College. He received his B.A. from the University of California at Berkeley, and his Ph.D. in economics from The Johns Hopkins University. He is the author of numerous articles and books on economics, and serves as Editor for the Geonomics Institute for International Economic Advancement monograph series.